An Overview of the Changing Role of the Systems Librarian: Systemic shifts

CHANDOS
INFORMATION PROFESSIONAL SERIES

Series Editor: Ruth Rikowski
(email: Rikowskigr@aol.com)

Chandos' new series of books are aimed at the busy information professional. They have been specially commissioned to provide the reader with an authoritative view of current thinking. They are designed to provide easy-to-read and (most importantly) practical coverage of topics that are of interest to librarians and other information professionals. If you would like a full listing of current and forthcoming titles, please visit our web site www.chandospublishing.com or email info@chandospublishing.com or telephone +44 (0) 1223 891358.

New authors: we are always pleased to receive ideas for new titles; if you would like to write a book for Chandos, please contact Dr Glyn Jones on email gjones@chandospublishing.com or telephone number +44 (0) 1993 848726.

Bulk orders: some organisations buy a number of copies of our books. If you are interested in doing this, we would be pleased to discuss a discount. Please email info@chandospublishing.com or telephone +44 (0) 1223 891358.

An Overview of the Changing Role of the Systems Librarian: Systemic shifts

EDITED BY
EDWARD IGLESIAS

Chandos Publishing

Oxford · Cambridge · New Delhi

Chandos Publishing
TBAC Business Centre
Avenue 4
Station Lane
Witney
Oxford OX28 4BN
UK
Tel: +44 (0) 1993 848726
Email: info@chandospublishing.com
www.chandospublishing.com

Chandos Publishing is an imprint of Woodhead Publishing Limited

Woodhead Publishing Limited
Abington Hall
Granta Park
Great Abington
Cambridge CB21 6AH
UK
www.woodheadpublishing.com

First published in 2010

ISBN:
978 1 84334 598 5

British Library Cataloguing-in-Publication Data.
A catalogue record for this book is available from the British Library.

Typeset by RefineCatch Limited, Bungay, Suffolk
Printed in the UK and the USA

Contents

About the authors

Huibin (Heather) Cai is the Information Technology Services Librarian at McGill University Library, Montreal, Canada. In her current position, she supports the library systems, including the Integrated Library System (Aleph 500), Link Resolver (SFX) and Meta-search Gateway (MetaLib). She was formerly Webmaster of Peking University Library, Beijing, China and editor and manager of O'Reilly's Beijing Office. She is the author of several articles in professional and scholarly journals and has given presentations at professional conferences. She holds a BEng in Electrical Engineering and an MLIS (University of British Columbia).

John Durno serves as the Head of Library Systems for the University of Victoria in British Columbia, Canada. He is part of the management team of the library, advising on strategic deployment of technology within the library, as well as overseeing operations in its systems unit. Prior to his current appointment, he worked as Project Coordinator and Acting Manager for the British Columbia Electronic Library Network, a province-wide consortium of post-secondary libraries, where his primary focus was on automating workflows relating to the procurement and ongoing management of provincial database licenses. He has written/co-written articles published in *Library Trends*, *IFLA Journal* and *Feliciter*, and has a long-standing involvement with the Access library technology conference, having at various times acted as presenter, program committee chair and Hackfest coordinator. He also serves as technical advisor on the Negotiations Resource Team of the Canadian Research Knowledge Network, a national content acquisition initiative.

Rene Erlandson is the Director of Virtual Services at the University of Nebraska Omaha. Virtual Services at UNO encompasses Library Systems, Electronic Resources, Web Development, Networking and Emerging Technologies. Prior to moving to Nebraska, Rene held positions at the University of Illinois Urbana-Champaign Library, the Library of Congress' Illinois Newspaper Project and Iowa State University Library.

Giovanna Frigimelica has been Secretary General of the Italian Library Association (AIB) since February 2009. She previously worked for the AIB from 2006 as librarian in the special library of the Association, in charge of following the publishing workflows of AIB monographs and journals, and of the marketing of promotional advertisement and sponsorship. She graduated in 2001 in Conservation of Cultural Heritage (LIS syllabus) from the Ca' Foscari University of Venice, then worked from 2001 to 2005 for an outsourcing agency as librarian in several libraries (mostly public) of Treviso and Venice provinces. Since 2000 she has cooperated with the board of the AIB website for the maintenance of several pages, and she maintains a personal website with online resources on LIS. Due to this interest, she has been a speaker at a number of training courses on library web design and Internet searching skills since 2004. She is also interested in technologies for libraries, in particular library automation software (ILS and OPAC).

Dan Gall is currently the Distance Education Librarian at the University of Iowa and has worked in distance education since 1998. After vowing in high school to never become a librarian, he got his MLIS from the University of Wisconsin in 1995 and has worked in public and academic libraries in Wisconsin, Botswana, Minnesota, Michigan and Iowa. Firmly rooted in the public service librarian tradition, Dan has found that his experience helping remote students overcome technological barriers to access library resources has made him deeply appreciate the 'geeks' he works with. He uses that term only with the utmost respect and wishes he were talented enough to be a geek himself. Intellectual curiosity is a trait Dan shares with most librarians and he truly enjoys the challenge of helping others research their areas of interest. Education is a ladder that allows individuals to improve their own lives and Dan's interest in distance education stems from a desire to help people who might not otherwise have access to education. He is also proud to be part of the University of Iowa's efforts to support minority and first generation college students on campus and is currently working on a pilot project to provide degree programs in Iowa prisons through distance education.

Denise A. Garofalo always wanted to be a librarian. She is currently the Systems and Catalog Services Librarian at Mount Saint Mary College in Newburgh, NY. She has previously served as Library Director at the Astor Home for Children (Rhinebeck, NY), and held various technology positions at the Mid-Hudson Library System, Poughkeepsie, NY (Automated Systems Manager, Director for Technology, Director for Telecommunications and Director for Communications Resources, and was Web Team Leader). Before returning to New York State, she was the Automation Consultant at the New Hampshire State Library (Concord, NH), Head of Technical Services and Automated Services at the Warwick Public Library (Warwick, RI), and a Librarian at the Pawtucket Public Library (Pawtucket, RI). She held various positions at the libraries at the State University of New York at Albany, and in high school worked after school and summers at the Perry Browne Elementary School Library (Norwich, NY). She has consulted with libraries on technology, information processing and digitization projects. She has served as an adjunct professor for over ten years at the Department of Information Studies at the State University of New York at Albany, teaching courses in information technology and information processing and organization. Denise is a trustee for the Marlboro Free Library in New York and has served on various library committees at the regional and state level. She has given presentations at state conferences as well as at the Internet Librarian and Computers in Libraries conferences. She reviews for *Library Journal, School Library Journal, American Reference Books Annual* and *Technical Services Quarterly*. She developed the website for the Heart of the Hudson Valley Farmers Market (Marlboro, NY).

Donna L. Hirst is currently Project Coordinator for Library Information Technology (LIT) at the University of Iowa. In this capacity she supervises and coordinates LIT projects, is liaison to IT vendors and user groups, and provides support in LIT financial management. Donna has co-authored with Paul Soderdahl numerous publications including 'The Core Competency Program at the University of Iowa Libraries', Chapter 8 of *Core Technology Competencies for Libraries and Library Staff*, ed. S. Thompson, New York: Neal Schuman Publishers. In 2003 she co-authored with Suzanne Julich and Brian Thompson 'A Case Study of ILS Migration: Aleph500 at the University of Iowa' (*Library Hi Tech* 21: 1: pp. 44–55). Donna has been active in the ELUNA Users Group and the North American Aleph Users Group serving as chair and past chair, and on the Steering Committee. On the university campus she has served on the University Staff Council, the

University Diversity Committee and the Academic Computer Services Committee.

Edward Iglesias is Systems Librarian at Central Connecticut State University. He has worked in a variety of library environments and has been interested in library technology since his first job as 'Special Projects Librarian' for a large law firm. Currently Edward is very interested in Next Generation Catalogs, the role of open source software in libraries and Creative Commons Licensing. He blogs regularly for ITIG, the Information Technology Interest Group of ACRL/New England.

Andrea Marchitelli was born in Rome, where he still lives, in 1975. He has been working in libraries since 1999, initially as a cataloguer, and later became involved in management. He is interested in new technologies, in particular those related to the WWW environment for libraries and electronic publishing. He works at CILEA (a non-profit consortium of Italian universities) as an information specialist, and is an employee of the Libraries and Electronic Publishing Services Section, which provides innovative solutions for electronic publishing and digital libraries using open-source and OAI-PMH-compliant software. Since 2003 Andrea has been Italian editor of E-LIS, the open archive for library and information science, and in 2009 he became a member of the IFLA IT Section Standing Committee. He teaches courses on electronic publishing and library automation (ILS, OPAC in particular) and in 2010 was appointed temporary professor of Informatic applications for libraries at the University of Bologna (Italy).

Lisa Carlucci Thomas is an experienced manager and librarian known for her leadership and innovation in academic libraries and for her research on mobile devices and e-books. Lisa is Digital Services Librarian at Southern Connecticut State University, where she is responsible for exploring, developing and coordinating library technologies, systems and digital initiatives. Lisa previously worked at the Yale University Library in the areas of digital collections, e-resource management, archives, reference and access services. She received her MLIS from the Syracuse University School of Information Studies, and was recently recognized by the American Library Association as a 2009 Emerging Leader. Lisa's column, 'Social Eyes', appears in the *Journal of Web Librarianship*.

Acknowledgements

This book is dedicated to my wife Paula Quenoy who has been an unending source of support and encouragement throughout not only the process of writing this book, but also all the years that led up to it.

Introduction

Edward Iglesias

This book grew out of the author's own experience at Central
Connecticut State University as a Systems Librarian. Starting
out, the role of the systems librarian had been a very traditional
one. The offices contained filing cabinets filled with computer
parts as well as old computers and monitors kept 'just in case'.
There were tools left over from the days when the Systems
Office did all of the network routing. There were two decrepit
Sun servers that had been bought years before when there was
money, only to find there was no way to upgrade them when
times became financially difficult. In short, it was a pretty
average situation.

In the following years it became apparent that much of the
old equipment and even the old skill sets were no longer
needed. Servers were now mostly concentrated in the campus
data center. All public computers as well as all network
infrastructure were bought and maintained by IT. Virtual
servers were the norm and automated network backups took
the place of having a staff member manually inserting backup
tapes. Even the skills needed to maintain the Integrated Library
System were different as Java-based clients replaced character-
based telnet sessions. This created a new set of challenges.
First, if the systems librarian was no longer in charge of
maintaining public and staff computers, what was the new

role? If servers were to be moved out of the library, who would maintain them? This position had an additional challenge in that Central Connecticut State University was part of a consortium that shared resources, including the ILS.

The solutions presented themselves but certain trends began to develop. There was an increase in outsourcing of what had been locally held databases. A great deal of the systems librarian's time was spent coordinating operations between the home library and other institutions, be they other libraries, other departments or vendors. Because of this focus a decision was made to merge two departments, Electronic Resources and Systems. This allowed one unit to handle nearly everything web-related that happened in the library. It also freed up the Electronic Resources Librarian from having to do a reference shift and information literacy classes, to devote herself to the increasing task of database management and web customization. In all it was a big win for the library. It also caused some confusion and resentment among staff more used to the old way of doing things. This is inevitable when major change happens but now the new department has been accepted.

This process of changing responsibilities and chains of command seemed logical and brought about the inevitable question of how other libraries were responding to change in the systems world. What follows is an attempt to answer this question from a wide-ranging set of viewpoints.

The first chapter, 'Digital culture: the shifting paradigm of systems librarians and systems departments' by Rene Erlandson is a good overview of the field and of how the specific role played by the systems librarian has evolved. In Chapter 2, 'Patchwork redux: how today's systems librarians enrich the weave of library culture,' Denise A. Garofalo takes a look at the more widely distributed responsibilities of the systems librarian in a team based library environment.

The third chapter, 'Library automation and open source software in Italy: an overview', provides a wonderful look into the historic role open source plays in Italian libraries and how it came about. 'Geeks and Luddites: library culture and communication' by Dan Gall and Donna Hirst follows this theme, focusing on a more anthropological view of library culture and the role systems play in it.

The second half of the book considers the current environment. My own chapter, 'The status of the field', offers a snapshot, by means of a survey, of some of the attitudes and morays present in the field as of 2009. Heather Cai's 'Building winning partnerships with vendors' looks at the increasing importance of dealing with vendor relations as well as how to form 'winning partnerships.' In 'Enterprise Computing and the Library: Managing the Transition,' John Druno focuses on the increasing role of Enterprise computing in the library and the accompanying change in mindset for the systems librarian. Finally, 'Doing more with more: systems, services and emerging technologies' by Lisa Carlucci Thomas is a great example of the enthusiasm and energy brought to the field by a new generation of systems librarians. Her insights represent a trending norm: someone who is a systems librarian but who uses more than just the system.

It is the author's hope that this book will be a good overview for students and researchers trying to make sense of this subset of the library profession. One of the common themes in several of the chapters is the need for better communication. This book is a start.

Edward Iglesias
Systems Librarian
Central Connecticut State University

Digital culture: the shifting paradigm of systems librarians and systems departments

Rene J. Erlandson

Introduction

The changing identity of libraries has been the topic of many articles and books in recent years. Most of these discourses center on the cultural shift from the traditional conceptual model of library as a place, to a vision of a library that defies physical and geographic boundaries. At the core of these discussions is the understanding that libraries are not static institutions. The shared cultural understanding or definition of 'library' has developed over time and will continue to evolve. Today, the library is at once a building, a collection, a staff, an assortment of services and a disembodied virtual entity. Are there correlations between the institution's evolution and the development of systems librarian positions and library systems departments? How have the cultural changes affecting libraries altered the role of systems librarians and library systems departments? What is the future for systems librarians? These are questions we will explore further.

Cultural evolution and development of system departments

In the 1970 edition of *Structure of Scientific Revolutions*, Thomas Kuhn postulated that scientific advancement is a 'series of peaceful interludes punctuated by intellectually violent revolutions', where 'one conceptual world view is replaced by another' (p. 10). Kuhn theorized that catalysts, or change agents, instigated the metamorphoses from one way of thinking to another. Paradigm shift catalysts embodied both previous knowledge and new discoveries which challenged previous or existing frameworks. During the twentieth century, the conceptual view of libraries as isolated place-based institutions underwent a revolutionary transformation to the library as an entity unrestrained by physical or geographic boundaries.

Prior to the 1960s, libraries were largely isolated. Collections were processed, housed and used locally. However, several catalysts would force libraries in the United States and the United Kingdom out of isolation into collaboration, and lead to the development of systems librarian positions and library systems departments. Two of these catalysts were the development of mainframe computers and the onset of an economic crisis.

The development of mainframe computers and their subsequent availability to large universities and municipalities in the United States and the United Kingdom during the 1960s led librarians in institutions with access to computer departments to begin exploring ways to harness the technology for use in libraries. As early as 1962, Marjorie Griffin predicted that one day there would be regional catalogs in the United States that would facilitate inter-library loans, including automatically generated ILL requests for items not found in local catalogs (Griffin, 1962).

In 1969, the Birmingham Libraries' Cooperative Mechanisation Project (BLCMP) was formed in the United Kingdom. Funded by a grant from the Office of Science and Technical Information, the project conducted an 18-month feasibility study of the cooperative use of machine-readable catalog (MARC) records at Aston University, the University of Birmingham and Birmingham Public Libraries. Additional grants were procured throughout the 1970s to study the feasibility of MARC record use for the automation of other library processes, like circulation (Stubley, 1988).

Economic stagnation combined with growing inflation in the United States during the 1970s caused funding problems for many libraries. As administrators struggled through the economic crisis, they looked for ways to reduce costs and increase efficiency. Institutions with multiple geographic locations, like colleges and universities, identified duplication of cataloging processes within libraries as one area where cost savings might be reaped, if work-flows could be combined and processes streamlined with automation. In addition, as budgets shrank librarians began exploring the possibility of systematic sharing of collections. The desire to decrease the costs associated with processing incoming library materials, coupled with the desire to decrease the capital spent on collections while still providing users with materials, combined with the availability of networked computer technology led to the development of consortia in the United States in places like California, Ohio and Illinois. Small groups of libraries began to partner with each other to use computer technology to automate library processes and develop union catalogs representing multiple institutions in multiple geographic areas. Formation of these partnerships in the United States and the United Kingdom began to erode the conceptual model of libraries as isolated institutions.

As library administrators made the decision to incorporate computer technology into traditional library operations in an effort to automate processes and cut costs, libraries needed staff to implement the technology. An examination of classified advertisements of open library positions from the American Library Association periodical, *Library Journal*, documents the impact technological implementation had on librarian positions in the United States throughout the last half of the twentieth century and into the next millennium.

The August 1964 issue of *Library Journal* included a position announcement by the St. Louis Public Library asking for a librarian 'to head technical processes in large public library ... with opportunity to explore library applications of data processing' (p. 3049). A later ad in the December 1, 1964 issue of *Library Journal* sought a 'Head Cataloger III' with the Suffolk Cooperative Library System in New York and stressed the 'opportunity to work with Univac 1004 and taped drive units; procedures automated' (p. 4830). In the March 1, 1965 issue of *Library Journal*, the University of Massachusetts Library notes in an advertisement for multiple technical services librarian positions 'Automation being studied' (p. 1206).

As library administrators in the United States and the United Kingdom targeted technical library processes for implementation of automation, technical services librarians and catalogers were given the opportunity to acquire technology skills that augmented the traditional technical services skill sets and principles taught in library science programs. These catalogers and technical services librarians who explored implementation of automated processes and incorporated computer technology into their daily routines and work-flows were functioning as early systems librarians.

During 1970, advertisements for open Computer Systems Analyst and Systems Analyst positions were found in *Library*

Journal. Systems-related positions were hired by libraries to manage the installation of cable and equipment that was needed to facilitate the technical services migration from paper-based processes to streamlined digital work-flows. In the February 15 issue of *Library Journal*, University of California Santa Cruz advertised for a Systems Analyst Librarian, which required an MLS. The position would oversee one programmer and five key punchers. However, not all positions required an MLS. In the January 15, 1970 issue of *Library Journal*, the Virginia State Library required only 'experience in library operations' (p. 180) for the open systems position they advertised.

Another catalyst in the paradigm shift of library culture, which also affected the development of library systems departments in the United Kingdom and the United States, was the creation and growth of library cooperatives and consortia. As mentioned earlier, the Birmingham Libraries' Cooperative Mechanisation Project (BLCMP) was formed in the United Kingdom in 1969. Throughout the 1970s additional grants were obtained to continue funding various applied technology studies for cooperative members. By 1977, the grant-funded initiative had developed into a fully independent entity, BLCMP Library Services Ltd. Libraries throughout the United Kingdom were able to obtain access to other computer-based housekeeping products by joining the cooperative. As libraries joined BLCMP, individuals within local libraries were assigned responsibility for implementing the new system (often within technical services) or additional positions were created to shoulder this responsibility (Warlow, 1994: 131).

In the United States, the Ohio College Library Center (OCLC) was organized in 1967. OCLC was born out of a desire by college and university administrators in the State of Ohio to reduce costs and share resources. However, the Ohio consortia quickly recognized the potential of joining with other consortia to develop a national endeavor and opened up membership beyond the geographic borders of Ohio. Within eight years of organizing, OCLC allowed several other library consortia to become co-operative members of the organization, including the New England Library Network, the Pittsburgh Regional Library Center, Federal Library Information Network, Amigos, PALINET, Missouri Library Network Corporation, Illinois Library & Information Network, Southeastern Library Network, Inc. and the State Universities of New York (OCLC, Inc., 2005).

The growth of OCLC in the United States corresponded to an increase of technology-based librarian positions across the nation. In the March 1, 1975 issue of *Library Journal*, the University of California advertised for a manager of the university-wide library automation program. Throughout 1976, eight automation-related positions were advertised in *Library Journal*, of which five advertisements listed required qualifications and all five included the MLS Libraries in Michigan and Indiana (both new OCLC members) were among those institutions advertising for an Assistant Network Coordinator and a Network Librarian, respectively.

In 1977, BLCMP in the United Kingdom moved from a grant-funded project to an autonomous organization. At the same time, OCLC in the United States changed its governance structure, opening up membership to all libraries in the United States (OCLC, Inc., 2009). Any library across the United States willing to invest in the infrastructure to communicate with OCLC could avail themselves of existing high-quality catalog records, thus reducing the amount of cataloging done locally. At the same time, the cost of the OCLC service could be off-set by uploading new original records into the OCLC online union catalog resulting in a credit for cataloging that would normally be done locally anyway. As additional libraries partnered with OCLC for online cataloging and resource sharing, an ever increasing number of library systems units were added to library organizational charts in the United States. Between the beginning of 1977 and the end of 1979, fourteen advertisements for open systems related positions were posted in *Library Journal*, not including cataloging positions that required MARC and OCLC experience, thirteen of which indicated an MLS was a job requirement. Early library systems departments were responsible for a relatively small number of dedicated terminals used predominantly by library staff for specific tasks, like accessing the national bibliographic utility used by the institution. As library card catalogs gave way to online public access catalogs (OPACs), library systems departments took on the responsibility for maintenance of still more dedicated terminals used by both library patrons and library staff. However, although the transition from a card catalog to a digital catalog resulted in the deployment of battalions of machines in libraries throughout the world, the primary responsibility of library systems departments remained narrowly focused on infrastructure installation and maintenance.

Throughout the decade of the 1980s, the number of library systems departments in the United States continued to grow as new technologies were released and incorporated into libraries. In August 1981, IBM introduced the personal computer with the MS-DOS operating system which greatly impacted businesses of all kinds, including libraries (Pollack, 1981). As PCs were implemented in libraries throughout the world, staff no longer needed to move from one machine to another to accomplish multiple tasks. Dedicated terminals gave way to multi-purpose machines hosting a number of individual software packages supported by library systems departments. By the end of the decade, many library OPACs gave way to integrated library systems (ILS). Formerly disparate digital processes like checking out a book, or checking in a journal, were joined together under the common umbrella of the ILS. Library staff were able to complete multiple processes in one digital environment. Library patrons could view the results of staff processing immediately, within one interface. At the same time, the Internet was becoming available to libraries associated with large research facilities, like universities, allowing communication and transfer of information to occur outside of dedicated cables/channels. The proliferation of computer systems added to libraries during the decade corresponded to an increase in the number of systems librarians (or similarly titled positions) being hired in libraries. By 1988, Budd notes 84 open systems librarian positions advertised in library journals in the United States. Once again, as technology became ever more pervasive in libraries, there was a corresponding increase in the number of institutions requiring the MLS for systems positions (78.6 percent) (Budd, 1990: 23 & 25).

The next major catalyst in the library paradigm shift also affected the development of systems librarian positions and library systems departments in the United States and the United Kingdom. The advent of the World Wide Web in 1991 and the development of graphical browsers like Mosaic and Netscape early in the decade opened up the world. During the last half of the 1980s, many libraries began allowing remote access to local library catalogs by users in an effort to facilitate identification and delivery of materials to patrons. However, with the development of HTML, libraries could now replicate collection materials and provide remote access to information contained within materials without ever routing the physical items to patrons. During the 1990s, libraries began to pilot digitization projects which would allow individuals to access library materials without ever visiting a library. Systems librarians began collaborating with other librarians to develop online finding aids, subject guides and digital collections.

During the decade of the 1990s, the skill set required of systems librarians in the United States also began to shift. In the United States, the role of systems librarians moved away from explicit technical skills, like programming and infrastructure installation, to focus on the broader principles of planning and development for integration of emerging technologies into libraries. In addition, responsibility for managing technically skilled library staff became an increasingly common role of systems librarians (Tyson, 2003: 317). Foote's examination of open position announcements for systems librarians found in library literature in the United States between 1990 and 1994 revealed over 82 percent of the advertisements reflected integrated library system management responsibilities along with a substantial number of administrative duties (Foote, 1997: 520). A survey sent to libraries in the United States during 1991 showed an increase in managerial responsibilities for systems librarians and an evolutionary separation of systems departments from technical services units (Leonard, 1993: 116). However, at the same time only 28 percent of systems librarians in the United Kingdom estimated that 50 percent or more of their responsibilities were 'non-IT' related (Muirhead, 1994, p. 11). Further content analysis of job advertisements for systems librarian positions later in the decade reveals that 'management-related' responsibilities, like planning and development, became increasingly important in these positions in the United States (Xu & Chen, 1999: 175). In addition, 82.7 percent of libraries advertising to fill open systems librarian positions in the United States between 1996 and 1997 required the MLS for employment in this capacity (Xu & Chen, 1999: 174). In the United Kingdom,

52.4 percent of systems librarians held a postgraduate diploma in L.I.S. (Muirhead, 1994: 17). As libraries became engaged in the creation of knowledge through online finding aids, subject guides, digital collections and more, the primary responsibility of systems librarian positions shifted from equipment caretaker to collaborator and manager.

In the first decade of this millennium, libraries were no longer geographically isolated, place-based institutions. Throughout the United States and the United Kingdom, library systems offices routinely provided network administration and support, acted as liaisons to electronic resource publishers, facilitated remote access to services and collections, coordinated resource sharing and document delivery, and initiated and coordinated digital collections and services while, in many cases, still maintaining responsibility for all institutional hardware/software and the ILS. Gradually over the previous three decades, as libraries incorporated technology into their operations, services and collections unrestrained by physical boundaries were created. At the same time as the library without walls evolved, systems librarians and library systems departments emerged as the caretakers, managers, architects and collaborators of the new library. By the end of the decade, individuals were able to locate information in collections all over the world, from anywhere in the world.

The future

Harvard University hosted a conference in 1949, where Donald Coney questioned the significance of libraries in academic institutions of the future (Coney, 1949). The debate over the relevancy of the library is not new. However, from the first known library at Elba in 1650 BC until today, the library as an institution has survived for more than 3000 years. History shows libraries are dynamic organizations. Over time, emerging technologies modified the identity and role of the library. Libraries continue to evolve. Because the cultural concept of the library is in a state of flux, constantly driven by emerging technology, the landscape in which systems librarians function is constantly shifting. It is important for systems librarians to recognize the transitional nature of their positions. As managers, systems librarians must understand the mission of the organizations they serve. Systems librarians must also have a holistic understanding of the profession. Knowledge of both the local organization and the profession will assist systems librarians in effectively uniting emerging technology with internal institutional and professional objectives. One of the most crucial elements of success for systems librarians as managers is to recruit and develop teams of flexible, well-informed, engaged staff. Library systems departments will not be able to predict and meet the needs of library users if library systems staff do not keep up with emerging trends and technologies. These responsibilities, coupled with the professional obligation of librarians to 'share their knowledge, skills and expertise with other institutions and associations,' supports the evolving trend by libraries to hire library systems staff and managers out of the ranks of library professionals (Goddard, 2003, p. 287).

Conclusion

When the development of systems librarian positions and library systems departments is examined within the context of the paradigm shift of libraries in our culture in the last half of the twentieth century, correlations are found. As library administrators identified ways to reduce costs associated with traditional library services by automating library processes using computers, individuals were needed to implement the new technology and create new work-flows.

The development of the World Wide Web in the early 1990s made it possible for libraries to provide services and collections to people around the world. As libraries began to provide remote access to services and collections, systems librarians became collaborators in creating discovery tools and knowledge bases. The complex, multi-faceted systems departments found in libraries in the United States and the United Kingdom today grew from the narrowly defined technical services positions and library units of the 1960s and 1970s. Library systems departments evolved from 'keepers of the machines' to teams of individuals responsible for collaborating to create virtual content and services, support current technologies and interpret emerging trends for library administrators (Tyson, 2003: 321).

As the culture of libraries shifted from isolated, place-based institutions to libraries without boundaries, individuals were needed to forecast, implement, support and guide the physical aspects of the virtual and ideological shift. Systems librarians and library systems departments have provided support for library objectives throughout the paradigm shift of library culture in recent decades.

The future of systems librarian positions and library systems departments is one of constant change. In order to successfully anticipate future needs, systems librarians and systems department staff must have a solid understanding of library processes and user practices. They must develop teams of flexible, well-informed staff. Systems librarians are a product of the paradigm shift of the library and will be substantive collaborators on the future library.

References

Budd, J. M. (1990). Salaries of automation librarians: Positions and requirements. *Journal of Library Administration, 13*(1/2), 21–9.

Coney, D. (1949). The future of libraries in academic institutions. *Harvard Library Bulletin* (Winter), 327–31.

Foote, M. (November 1997). The systems librarian in U.S. academic libraries: A survey of announcements from college and research libraries news, 1990–1994. *College and Research Libraries, 58*(6), 517–26.

Goddard, L. (2003). The integrated librarian: IT in the systems office. *Library Hi Tech, 21*(3), 280–8.

Griffin, M. (1962). The library of tomorrow. *Library Journal, 87*(8), 1555–7.

Kuhn, T. S. (1970). *The structure of scientific revolutions* (2nd enl. ed.). Chicago, Ill.: University of Chicago Press.

Leonard, B. G. (Spring 1993). The role of the systems Librarian/Administrator: A preliminary report. *Library Administration & Management, 7*(?), 113–16.

Muirhead, G. (1994). Systems librarians in the UK: The results of a survey. In G. Muirhead (Ed.), *The systems librarian: The role of the library systems manager*. London: Library Association Publishing, 3–46.

OCLC, Inc. (2005). *OCLC annual report. 2004–2005. OCLC timeline.* Retrieved November 12, 2009, from *http://library.oclc.org/u?/p267701coll28,162.*

OCLC, Inc. (2009). *History of OCLC.* Retrieved December 2, 2008, from *http://www.oclc.org/about/history/default.htm.*

Pollack, A. (1981). Big I.B.M.'s little computer. *New York Times*, D1. Retrieved from ProQuest Historical Newspapers The New York Times 1851–2006 database.

Stubley, P. (1988). *BLCMP: A guide for librarians and systems managers*. Aldershot, Hants, England; Brookfield, Vt: Gower.

Tyson, L. (2003). Library systems teams – more than just peripherals. *Library Hi Tech, 21*(3), 317–24.

Warlow, A. (1994). More by accident than design, or, the rise and rise of a chief cataloguer? In G. Muirhead (Ed.), *The systems librarian: The role of the library systems manager*. London: Library Association Publishing, 129–45.

Xu, Hong and Hsin-liang Chen. (June 1999). What do employers expect? The educating systems librarian research project 1. *The Electronic Library, 17*(3), 171–8.

2

Patchwork redux: how today's systems librarians enrich the weave of library culture

Denise A. Garofalo

Technology developments and economic changes have combined to provide the momentum for the redesign of the perception of today's libraries. Fortunately, the core mission of libraries remains the same – meeting the information needs of our users. But the fundamental duties of system librarians have been re-shaped and redefined, a reflection of the changes that are occurring in the realm of digital technology, a technology that has become the means for libraries to fulfill their core mission. Traditional service models may still be critical in some areas, but as libraries rely more and more on digital technology to provide vital library functions, systems librarians are even more important in helping to ensure that libraries and their staff are equipped to successfully survive the ongoing transformation.

As today's libraries struggle to deal with the shifting information landscape while meeting the varying information needs of library users, systems librarians have become increasingly critical to seamless and successful library technology projects. Whereas in the past systems departments and systems librarians were seen as a bridge between the library and the 'techies,' in today's collaborative culture it is the systems librarian, as information technology professionals and not just 'PC-fix-it' librarians, who have influenced and championed the transformations that have resulted in an improved technology comfort zone for libraries.

The world has changed since those early days of systems librarians as technology fix-it people. The systems librarian of that day built the technology infrastructure in whatever fashion and by whatever means were available, and was very much involved in using technical skills as a computer professional, showing that librarians can work side by side with technically-trained computer staff and trailblazing the path for today's systems librarians as technology managers. Essentially the systems librarian has been transformed into an information professional who combines skills and knowledge in librarianship with information technology, with a liberal dose of solid interpersonal relationship skills. The transformation systems librarians have undergone results in an effective manager who can implement those technology projects and maintain those technology initiatives that support the library's mission.

No matter the title (automation librarian, systems manager, technology manager, etc.), the need for a librarian to be responsible for the technology that made its way into the library has not changed. What has changed is the way that the person or persons responsible for the technology is viewed by the library management, library staff and administrative authorities. Twenty years ago the awareness that libraries even had technology needs may have been unknown to a library's school district, college administration, or municipal or other authority. And the concept that libraries should be included in an institution's long-range technology planning efforts just was not considered. Fortunately, as time has progressed the entities with fiscal responsibilities and authority over libraries have realized that including the library and its needs in technology planning is essential.

It is more likely to find today's systems librarians meeting with their city's or college's IT department to plan for an upcoming hardware upgrade than continuing as the librarian who can fix screaming hard drives while leaping over co-ax cable to troubleshoot routers. As libraries become more entrenched as a digital information service point, systems librarians are key innovators and implementers in the process to keep the library current and critical to today's users. This transformation, though, did not occur in a vacuum but was rather a slow and steady outgrowth of the evolution of the library itself. Systems librarians have served as a lynchpin in altering the way libraries perceive technology.

Libraries in the late twentieth century were essentially buildings that warehoused books. As the information age grew and spread, technology invaded the library, aiding and abetting how libraries operated, usually without any cohesive plan on how best to utilize it. An alteration had to occur in the library's perception of just what a library was. When libraries stopped viewing themselves as book repositories that happened to have some computers (but only where absolutely required!) but instead embraced the perspective that computers were just another tool to use to meet library users' information needs, it was the systems librarians who were in place as the information professionals best equipped to shepherd and support this paradigm shift.

The connected mindset pervading the world as a whole is not new to the library world. Library culture fosters such connectedness, supporting the need for networking with other librarians and library staff. Systems librarians have that same need to remain connected, not only to the library world but to the technology world, to stay abreast of the emerging technologies and how they will impact the library. Systems librarians stay connected with their peers through listservs, various associations and conferences and other networks, since these contacts are useful when planning, troubleshooting or working on technology projects. Librarians as a whole have also been keen to stay in touch with each other and network, attend conferences and connect with other librarians for decades. These past decades of societal change, driven by technology and what it allows people to do, have truly changed the way libraries do business, highlighting the need for a library professional to maintain awareness of new technologies and how they can be used to support the mission of the library – meeting the information needs of the user.

Today libraries are finding ways to integrate Web 2.0 tools and concepts into the reboot referred to as Library 2.0. Many of these Library 2.0 concepts describe the focus of today's system librarian – collaboration, sharing, flexibility, with a user-focused outlook. Technology today enhances the user's library experience and expands access to information. Library automation has changed library services and library culture over the years. From the online catalog to the CD-ROM network to resource sharing networks to today's convenient remote access to information sources, systems librarians have learned how to navigate each new development's environment and how to bring these changes into their library with the least disruption. By so doing systems librarians have elicited positive changes in the very culture of libraries and library staff members.

Attempting to define and highlight the manner in which the culture of libraries has been changed, influenced and reworked to become the fabric of today's library culture relies on a clear conception of what is meant by an organization's culture.

> Organizational culture is manifested in the typical characteristics of the organization, in other words,

organizational culture should be regarded as the right way in which things are done or problems should be understood in the organization (Sun, 2008: 137).

Logically, it then follows that library culture is best described as the correct way to do things or solve problems within a library. With both the 'Web 2.0' mindset and the integration of technology-solving characteristics brought into the library from systems librarians and systems staff, it only makes sense that library culture would contain aspects of both within the everyday operations, concepts and behaviors. Deciding to set up a campaign to change an organization's culture can be problematic, since culture is fluid and difficult to compartmentalize (Linn, 2008: 91). But when change is subtle and comes from within, a result more of influence and observation than of a mandate, culture can be modified over time. The effect of systems librarians on library culture is unassuming but significant.

In this digital age, social networking is the current latest and greatest trend. Collaboration and team work go hand in hand with the current influence of social networking. Systems librarians have been involved in aspects of social networking from the beginning. With the successful completion of a project as the goal, systems librarians work with colleagues and will collaborate with whomever necessary in order to meet that goal. Collaborating with technology vendors, IT departments/staff members, telecommunications vendors, suppliers and fellow systems librarians is not just second nature to systems librarians, it is a necessary ability. Yesterday's email lists are enhanced by today's blogs and wikis, but the benefit is the same – working together, sharing information and striving to instill a sense of teamwork. These same concepts that have been characteristic of successful systems librarians for years are now used to articulate the features of the twenty-first-century successful library culture.

Libraries had been demonstrating successful collaborative work for a large part of the twentieth century. Coordinated collection development, shared cataloging resources and resource sharing through interlibrary loan networks are just some of the better-known and longer-lasting indicators of libraries' collaborative culture. Some academic and large research libraries are collaborating with scholars in the rapidly developing faction for free online scholarship and institutional repositories of scholarship. The Google Books project and subsequent litigation are examples of a collaborative venture that has not yet been resolved in a positive light, but still it underscores the facet of library culture that embraces the opportunity to work together with others towards a shared goal or ideal.

Twenty-first-century libraries have access to an abundance of information, sources and resources that are digital, traditional and everything in between. Successful contemporary libraries are differentiated by the range, recognition and reputation of the quality of the service provided to library users; if users can access the information they desire then the library is seen as successful. The essential change that underpins achieving this success relies on library staff members working together as a team. The traditional hierarchical structure gives way to a flattened formation, and results in a work culture where the library customer's needs and expectations become the focus of the library workers' efforts, and where management supports problem-solving and collaborative planning over traditional reporting sequences and supervision. This change in perspective in the culture of libraries parallels the existing culture of technologically advanced staff, a culture that seeped into the library world from a variety of sources but was nurtured by systems librarians.

Whether out of necessity or serendipitously, systems librarians and systems staff have become accustomed to the teamwork approach. When a technology project needs to be completed, systems librarians coordinate the necessary experts required to get the tasks done, whether they are the city's IT department, the school's technology consultant, the college's IT staff, other library staff, technology vendors or training providers. The systems librarian involves anyone with knowledge of or a stake in seeing the successful completion of a technology project to discuss, plan, troubleshoot and strategize the approach to achieve the desired result.

As work cultures overall began turning towards team building, libraries were better positioned to implement a collaborative work culture because systems librarians and systems offices had already introduced 'team think' into library culture. Because of the often varied circumstances in which technology has been introduced into libraries, the systems office, staff and librarians took advantage of the benefits that working as a team can bring. Although useful for all aspects of library activities, building strategic relationships is essential for systems staff. Whether it is partnerships with an IT department or cooperative relationships with other libraries (Tyson, 2003: 318), systems librarians forge alliances across departments, libraries and organizations, regardless of distance, with the simple laser-like focus on the goal of successfully completing the project.

Perhaps because libraries traditionally have had to operate at times with a less than ideal financial reservoir, that collaboration across department barriers and across institutional boundaries has forced libraries to be accepting of the systems librarians' idea, proven through experience, that the larger the pool of skills and knowledge available to focus on a issue, the better the chance to find a solution.

Building effective teams that are encouraged to share ideas in an open and supportive environment results in innovative solutions to issues and problems; the experience of systems librarians in planning and implementing technology projects over the years supports this perspective.

Not all libraries have systems librarians, but the need for someone who can provide the expertise to manage the technology and technical staff is common across the spectrum of libraries. There is a need for someone in the library to keep current with technology developments within the library world as well as within the greater technology universe. Twenty years ago a systems librarian would have been expected to find ways to use the donated Apple IIe, make sure the dot-matrix printer was outputting the overdue notices, and ensure the dial-up connection to OCLC was operational. However, today the expectation is to help the library and staff manage the changing technology rather than personally keep the technology operational; knowing who to contact to repair it rather than to personally make the repair. Systems librarians need to know *who* to contact about an issue, problem or project rather than know *what* to do to fix what is wrong.

Because of the differences in funding, governance, and staffing among the various types of libraries, it is difficult to describe a typical library or a typical systems librarian. Nonetheless, there are certain similarities amongst them all. Each library must solve the technology problems that they encounter according to the plans they have in place. It is unusual to find a library with a non-librarian information technology professional assigned to manage the library's technology, and even today there are many libraries dealing with their technology needs without a library professional in the role of systems librarian. Perhaps these situations exist due to the belief that the technology is driving and controlling the change in libraries rather than being the stimulus. It appears that the more often the perception held of systems librarians is aligned with innovative implementers, the better the library is poised to accept technology and change (Starr, 2009).

Work environments overall have changed in the last twenty years. Library culture has also changed. The move toward inclusive teams that cross traditional departmental borders and shared decision-making, results in a better customer-centered culture. Systems librarians have had to work in teams from varied types of organization, such as IT centers or municipal or school technology departments, crossing barriers and functional boundaries in order to ensure the success of library technology initiatives. The collaboration, interoperation and distributed workflow that resulted from the trailblazing of systems librarians have spread throughout the library. Successful libraries have always known that the client or library user is the center, and therefore focus on the needs of the library users. These libraries also have integrated interoperability, teams and collaboration in ways that continue to keep the user at the forefront of operations. The organizational culture of these libraries was receptive to these changes, no doubt because they had integrated key components of a successful organizational or library culture – 'trust and trustworthiness, empowerment and delegation, consistency and mentorship' (Kane-Urrabazo, 2006: 190).

Libraries strive towards competencies for staff. Specific competencies for systems librarians are not adequately delineated, as they vary from library type to institution and situation. Most systems librarians today did not receive training in how to perform their duties while studying to become a librarian; in fact, most of those librarians who have received an advanced degree geared toward systems librarianship are more likely to be working in a position outside of a library:

> More and more, librarians apply their information management and research skills to arenas outside of libraries – for example, database development, reference tool development, information systems, publishing, Internet coordination, marketing, Web content management and design, and training of database users. Entrepreneurial librarians sometimes start their own consulting practices, acting as freelance librarians or information brokers and providing services to other libraries, businesses, or government agencies. (US Bureau of Labor Statistics, 2009)

Nonetheless, all librarians today use technology in some way to manage information in all its formats to help library users find and access the information they need. Systems librarians are just generally more in tune and lead the way with the technology trends and impending changes and can communicate these to library staff and colleagues.

With the growing dependency of libraries on technology in order to function, it is indeed fortunate that systems librarians and systems staff are available to aid libraries in coming to terms with these changes. But just what factors are needed for the development of a successful systems librarian? Is it circumstances, training or a particular curiosity or mindset?

> There are people who are mentally wired to think outside the box. They think in the big picture and in detail, sometimes simultaneously, and aren't afraid to stand up to convention. Those who develop the skill sets that navigate through group dynamics and make change happen are leaders and change agents. (Starr, 2009)

The future of libraries is bound to information technology. In those instances where systems librarians have flourished and been able to integrate positive changes in library culture the libraries will be best positioned to cope with whatever else is in store for us. Hopefully library culture will be able to take on the next great challenge: how to remain relevant in a world where technology is so all-pervading. Libraries are not the only ones involved in information access today, and systems librarians graduating with advanced degrees are finding enhanced employment opportunities outside libraries, a trend that if unabated would be detrimental to libraries overall.

Libraries have benefited from the influence of systems librarians and systems staff on the overall culture of libraries. The widespread embracing of the team approach to the work environment, the integration of information technology into the essence of meeting the library users' needs, and the continued utilization of networking to supplement and enhance how librarians do their work are just a few of the subtle influences systems librarians have had on libraries. The coming years will only continue the enhanced role of systems librarians in the development of the libraries of the future. The combination of specialized knowledge in information technologies with the knowledge of librarianship, plus their collaborative and team-building skills will continue to result in a crucial role for systems libraries.

References

Boule, Michelle. (2008). 'Best Practices for Working in a Virtual Team Environment.' *Library Technology Reports* 44 (1), 28–31. *Academic Search Premier*, EBSCO*host* (accessed October 4, 2009).

'Essential Skills of a Tech Chief.' (2005). *School Library Journal, 51* (5), 44. *Academic Search Premier*, EBSCO*host* (accessed October 4, 2009).

Goddard, Lisa. (2003). 'The integrated librarian: IT in the systems office.' *Library Hi Tech, 21* (3), 280–88.

Hatcher, Karen A. (1995). 'The Role of the Systems Librarian/ Administrator: A Report of the Survey.' *Library Administration & Management, 9* (2), 106–9.

Kane-Urrabazo, Christine. (2006). 'Management's role in shaping organizational culture.' *Journal of Nursing Management, 14* (3), 188–94. *Academic Search Premier*. EBSCO (accessed October 19, 2009).

Lavagnino, Merri Beth. (1997). 'Networking and the Role of the Academic Systems Librarian: An Evolutionary Perspective'. *College & Research Libraries*, May, 217–31.

'Librarian – career, jobs, salary.' *Articles.DirectoryM.com – Everything you need to know. It's just that easy! http:// articles.directorym.com/Librarian-a861737.html#8075069* (accessed October 14, 2009).

Linn, Mott. (2008) 'Organizational Culture: an Important Factor to Consider.' *The Bottom Line, 21* (3), 88. ABI/ INFORM Global, ProQuest. Web (accessed October 14, 2009).

Martin, S. K. (1988). 'The Role of the Systems Librarian.' In Downes, R. ed. *Computing, Electronic Publishing and Information Technology: Their Impact on Academic Libraries*. New York: Haworth Press. 57–68.

Rhyno, Arthur. (2003) 'From Library Systems to Mainstream Software: How Web Technologies are Changing the Role of the Systems Librarians.' *Library Hi Tech, 21*(3), 289–96.

Starr, Karen J. (2009) 'Systems Librarians as Change Agents?' Message to the author. October 22, 2009. Email.

Sun, Shili. (2008) 'Organization Culture and Themes.' *International Journal of Business and Management*, 3 (12), 137–41.

Tyson, Lisa. (2003) 'Library Systems Teams – More than Just Peripherals.' *Library Hi Tech*, 21 (3), 317–24.

U.S. Bureau of Labor Statistics (2009). 'Librarians. *http://www.bls.gov/oco/ocos068.htm#nature* (accessed October 14, 2009).

3

Library automation and open source software in Italy: an overview

Giovanna Frigimelica and Andrea Marchitelli

The notions of information technology and procedure automation started to circulate within Italian libraries at the end of the 1960s, when the first software products were released for that use. The turning point was 1968, as a result of a tragic event in Italian history: the flooding of Florence in 1966. In October 1968 a seminar was held in Florence to present the results of two studies carried out in the framework of the aid from ALA to Italian libraries: John Finzi from the Library of Congress and Joseph Becker of EDUCOM dealt with the possibility of reorganizing in a new way the services offered by the Central National Library of Florence.

The conclusions of the seminar were various. The first was a study on information technologies and the formal usage of the MARC standard, with the program ANNA.[1] After a short time, the 'Biblio' project was started in order to support the automation of the Central National Library of Rome. In the same year the university consortia, originally established to support supercomputing, started to play a significant role in university library automation.

Although the automation of BNI (Italian National Bibliography) has been an important step in the process of library automation, the process had no direct practical consequences, because the Italian library system itself, lacking in real catalographic cooperation, considered BNI an authoritative source for catalographic control rather than for derived cataloguing.[2]

In the 1970s the experimentation involved the documentation centres of important research institutes such as CNR (National Research Council), CNEN (Nuclear Energy Commission) and ISS (National Institute for Health).[3] These experiments focused attention on internal procedures, such as acquisition and cataloguing, rather than on services to users, such as document circulation. This approach, caused by careful planning and scarcity of funds, would have as a consequence the constant delay of services to the public.

At the end of the 1970s a cooperation project at a national level appeared, providing the basis for the interlibrary loan service, SNADOC, which is the forerunner of SBN, the Italian National Library Service. The project, based on the idea of creating a cooperative 'service', ambitiously aimed to create 'a new drawing of the Italian library situation'[4] rather than to rationalize the internal management procedures.

The elaboration of SBN began in 1980 – with further proposals being strongly criticized in 1985, while the system eventually saw the light in 1992 when the two Central National Libraries (Rome and Florence) facilitated the connection to the Index processor, at the heart of the information architecture.[5] In more recent years the technological changes have been so radical that the Index appeared to be outdated, a true legacy of the prevailing client-server software framework. However, SBN could not bridge the delay: the decision in

2004 to create a client-server system, Unix-based, was accomplished in 2009, when a client-server architecture made way for web-based architectures.

The creation of SBN and its specific characteristics have played an important role in the Italian software market. The technological choices resulting from a feasibility study on SBN devolved by Italsiel and Geac, including the use of an IBM platform to manage the Index, and the utilization of SNA net protocol rather than ISO/OSI standard, caused a closure of the system on the structure of bibliographic data, on the hardware and communication protocols, and on conversation between the Index and the Poles.

Some Italian regions, such as Lombardy, Piedmont and Emilia-Romagna, played a leading role in SBN growth, funding the development of software packages, the management of which they entrusted completely or partially to private businesses (CSI Piemonte, Lombardia Informatica, Celcoop Ravenna), with the addition of Italsiel, creating a protected market without competition. Following agreement between the Italian state and these regions,[6] the software could be used for free by other regions who asked for it. This decision had the following consequences:[7]

- the absence of real competition blocked the proper development of a national market;

- separation of the institutional policies of a public organization from the commercial ones of the related private business became impossible.

The immobility of the market and the impossibility to choose freely between concurrent software hampered the development of quality software, limiting many Italian private businesses to the role of integrating gaps and a lack in the legacy software SBN.

In order to solve these problems and to adjust SBN to the current technologies, ICCU in 1996 entrusted Etnoteam to make a feasibility study on the evolution of SBN.[8]

The project 'Evolution of SBN Index' had a number of objectives:

- technological renewal of Unix-based hardware and software, use of TCP/IP protocol and of middleware market standard, object-programming, use of XML and UNICODE;

- rationalization, integration and structuring of the database;

- opening of the SBN Index to non-SBN library systems using the most common bibliographic formats, such as UNIMARC and MARC21, with the help of a standard interface allowing developers to provide other software access to the Index;

- management of different cooperation levels: each Pole could choose its own level of participation to SBN (data collection, location of possessed material, insertion of new catalographic descriptions, correction);

- development of new features, such as derived cataloguing (the possibility to import bibliographic data from different databases) and batch import (dumping of bibliographic archives previously built with comparison of data).

The first part of the project ended in February 2004, with the activation of Index2 SBN. From that time, the certification of software from different producers started: a certification of data flow and data stream between those applications and SBN Index is now required. This fact undoubtedly shook ILS's Italian market, keeping SBN at the core of the interests of developers with an out-and-out objective of certification.

SBN strongly influenced the library automation market, creating a dichotomy between SBN libraries and non-SBN libraries. Until the 1990s (and still today in some small establishments), different automation systems coexisted in the same library to manage different activities. Both international and locally developed software found a niche in the marketplace, offering tools to libraries that allowed the development of services to patrons different from SBN (in which great attention had always been paid to the cataloguing process).

Economic factors influenced this area: due to the scarce economic resources for libraries, developments had always been limited, the market stagnant, and the diffusion of advanced and expensive software narrowed.

The use of open source software for library management concerns few libraries at the moment, and there is no movement for the promotion of this school of thought. A study of April 2009[9] underlines that about twenty Italian libraries use open source library automation systems, against a total of 15 000 libraries in Italy.

PMB counts 13 installations, Koha 2, and Openbiblio only 1. Two more open source programs for OPAC developed in Italy, Jopac2 and Pico, are available. The libraries using OS library automation systems belong to private organizations, to schools or to the Church; these libraries are the weak link within the national system, which is very complex due to the fact that a variety of bodies manage it.[10] Libraries using the OS automation system receive no funding at all or have an inadequate budget, and usually their information and cultural function is not clearly recognized by the management of the Institution they belong to.

The diffidence towards open source in Italian libraries is now usually due to the fact that these products are unreliable and without a solid distributor or vendor to back them up. But in the history of library automation in our country we can find some important and well-known examples of software developed without distributors, and attempts to elaborate native open source software or to release the sources of proprietary software.

CDS/ISIS, a software developed and freely distributed from UNESCO (in collaboration with many other organizations), starting from 1985, is distributed in Italy by the DBA Association. In 2004, DBA declared 1800 distributions against 1500 the previous year.[11] Obviously, a distribution does not mean an active and working installation, but CDS/ISIS has been used by many public libraries, thanks to ad hoc applications made for the management of library processes.

The only Italian project for an open source ILS is DAFNE, born in 1999 within the provincial library system of Rovigo (Northern Italy). The source has never been released.[12]

Another example is @UOL, created in 1990 at the National Library of Florence with the partnership of Bassilichi. In 2005 it was announced that its source files would be made available with a LGPL licence – on single files, not on the whole of the software. To date, only one organization has asked for the source files, despite the usage of @UOL in the whole national territory (645 libraries, eight library systems with 359 libraries with @UOL installations in 2007).[13] The library system of the province of Bergamo (216 libraries) asked for the source files and, with the help of the Polytechnic Innovation Consortium of Milan (now Alintec), created a new proprietary software called B-Evolution.

There are two Italian projects dedicated to open source software development for library automation, both focusing on data publication into an OPAC: JOpac and PicO. JOpac2 started to be developed in 2000 by Romano Trampus and Albert Caramia. Based on their experience at the University of Trieste, Technology for Libraries department, they decided to create an open source software on a framework that made it easy to integrate data from different sources and to display it in different ways.[14] PicO (Primary Interface for Opac) is a tool for OPAC building created by CILEA on the basis of the software 'wwwisis', using the web environment of CD/ISIS. Its distribution is under a GNU GPL licence.[15]

Italy lacks a movement in favour of open source ILS: the few Italian projects seen before were not supported by institutions, and had often been completed without proper support and discouraging collaboration with the professional community (for example, by setting limits such as the need to ask for source files). Even in the professional literature we can find only a few articles about ILS open source.[16] These facts reflect the lack of interest in the diffusion of the open source movement in Italian libraries.

If we take a look to what happens outside Italy, we can see that in the United States in 2007, open source contracts represented 10 per cent of the ILS contracts for academic and public libraries.[17] In Belgium 51 libraries use an open source ILS among more or less 500 existing (i.e. 10 per cent).[18] In France one in every three libraries chooses an open source ILS.[19]

In the period between 2006 and 2008 a few Italian library systems faced re-computerization using a proprietary software. The reasons for the choice of proprietary software rather than open source ones, as gathered from informal talks by colleagues involved, were that the OS product is unsettled, and open source software means strong reliance on systems and information engineers.

The adoption of open source software for library automation can now, finally, respond to an instruction issued by the Italian Minister of Innovation and Technologies on 19 December 2003 on 'Development and Use of Information Software for Public Administrations': public administration should prefer information software that does not derive from a sole supplier or proprietary technology.

CILEA, one of most important Italian academic consortia for library automation, started distributing Koha at the end of 2009. Koha is one of the best-known open source ILS products and it is used by important libraries worldwide. It will be interesting to see how the Italian professional community respond to this new product. Since the lack of economic resources is chronic in Italian libraries, we doubt that the present economic crisis will turn libraries' attention towards open source systems. We need a cultural and management change: Italian libraries should plan their automation choices in a different way.

Notes

1. In 1975 the annual BNI (the Italian National Bibliography) catalogue was produced on magnetic tape; this was the first electronic processing of bibliographic data in Italy. Data was registered in a format resulting from modifications of both MARC II and UKMARC–ANNAMARC (Automazione Nella NAzionale, i.e. 'National Library Automation'). BNI was published in that format until 1984, when it started to use UNIMARC.
2. Weston, P.G., 2001. *Catalogazione bibliografica: dal formato MARC a FRBR*. 'Bollettino AIB', 41(3), 267–86.
3. Carosella, M.P. and Valenti, M., eds, 1973. *Progetti di automazione nelle biblioteche italiane*. Roma: AIB.
4. Crocetti, L., 1986. *Relazione introduttiva, La cooperazione: il Servizio Bibliotecario Nazionale*. Atti del 30. Congresso Nazionale della Associazione Italiana Biblioteche, 21–24 novembre 1982, Università di Messina.
5. The information component of SBN was designed between 1980 and 1985, with the aim of creating two main services: access to documents through a common catalogue of bibliographic resources of the main Italian libraries, and a national service for document circulation and loan. Both services are satisfied with the presence of a specific machine

called 'Index', which contains the basic elements to check a bibliographic notice and to address a specific request (loan, copy of a bibliographic record) to the most suitable library or database. Moreover, libraries belong to local systems called 'Poles', connected to the Index. The connection is kept working with the same procedures, even though sometimes based on different hardware. This solution respected the characteristics of the Italian market, divided into IBM; Olivetti, controlled by Carlo De Benedetti since 1978; Honeywell, who bought out the information activities of General Electrics in 1970 – including the Italian partner that became HISI (Honeywell Information Systems Italia), then Honeywell-Bull, and Bull, eventually; Sperry, bought by Burroughs in 1986, becoming Unisys Corporation. (Leombroni, C., 2003. *Una vicenda controversa: l'automazione delle biblioteche in Italia*, A. Petrucciani and P. Traniello, eds. In: *La storia delle biblioteche: temi, esperienze di ricerca, problemi storiografici*, 16–17 settembre 2002 2003, AIB pp. 167–96.)

6. Istituto Centrale per il Catalogo Unico e le informazioni bibliografiche, 1988. Convenzione tra il Ministero per i Beni e le Attività Culturali – tramite l'Istituto Centrale per il Catalogo Unico – e le Regioni Emilia-Romagna, Lombardia e Piemonte per lo scambio dei software SBN e la concessione in uso dei software medesimi alle altre Regioni o ad altri soggetti.

7. Leombroni, C., 2003. *L'automazione delle biblioteche italiane e l'SBN*. 'Economia della Cultura. Rivista dell'Associazione per l'Economia della Cultura', (3), 335–42.

8. Cerone, F. and Molfese, S., 1998. *Studio di fattibilità sull'evoluzione della rete SBN*. 'SBN Notizie', 1.

9. Frigimelica, G., 2009. 'La diffusione di software Open Source per la gestione di biblioteche in Italia'. 'Biblioteche oggi', 2009, vol. 27, n. 6, pp. 37–43, *http://eprints.rclis.org/17095/*.

10. Guerrini, M., 2009. *Libraries in Italy: a brief overview*; with the collaboration of G. Frigimelica. 'IFLA Journal', 35, n. 2, pp. 94–116.

11. Bertini, V., 2009. Rapporto sui sistemi di automazione in Italia 2005–2007, in *Rapporto sulle biblioteche italiane 2007–2008*, a cura di Vittorio Ponzani, Roma, AIB, pp. 115–27.

12. Sturman, R. 2004. *Il software open source per la gestione*

integrata delle biblioteche: una nuova risorsa?, 'Bollettino AIB', 44, 3, pp. 257–70, *http://www.aib.it/aib/boll/2004/0403257.htm.*

13. Bertini, op. cit.
14. *http://www.jopac2.org*
15. *http://www.cilea.it/index.php?id=931*
16. Only four articles can be found in the Italian professional literature: Frigimelica, op. cit., Sturman, op. cit., Di Giammarco, F. 2005. Open source e biblioteche: un incontro possibile. 'Biblioteche Oggi' vol. 26 (2005) n. 1, pp. 68–9; Baldi, P. 2005. Il bibliotecario e l'open source. 'Bibelot', a. 11 n. 2, *http://www .aib.it/aib/sezioni/toscana/bibelot/0502/b0502b.htm.*
17. Breeding, M. 2008. The Viability of Open Source ILS, 'Bulletin of the American Society for Information Science and Technology', 35, 2, pp. 20–5, *http://www.asis.org/Bulletin/ Dec-08/DecJan09_Breeding.html.*
18. Chalon, P., Melon, P., 2008. Les SIGB libres en Belgique: état des lieux et analyse, 'Cahiers de la documentation = Bladen voor documentatie' 2008/2, *http://eprints.rclis.org/14411/1/ chalon-melon_2008.pdf.*
19. Maisonneuve, M., 2008. Bibliothèques, l'équipement informatique en 2008, 'Livres Hebdo', 767 (2009), pp. 74–80, *http://www.livreshebdo.fr/cache/upload/pdf/enquete_tosca_ 2008.pdf.*

4

Geeks and Luddites: library culture and communication

Dan Gall and Donna Hirst

Introduction

The modern history of technological change has significantly influenced library culture. With this cultural evolution communication between systems staff and other librarians has changed as well. In this chapter the alpha geek and the Luddite archetypes are used to illustrate these tensions over the years. Current library culture mirrors the culture at large with ever increasing needs for effective communication by the systems librarian. In the twenty-first-century library the pervasive culture is user-driven and clearly influenced by spontaneous communication technologies like wikis and blogs that put more control in the hands of library users. In order to maximize their effectiveness, systems librarians must become more collaborative in their interpersonal styles and must increase their public face, roles which have been historically limited or prohibited.

Definitions

Although the topic of library culture is a serious one and worthy of consideration, please understand that this chapter considers the perceptions of various librarian roles – perceptions that can often be difficult to pin down. The use of slang terms like 'alpha geek' may add an element of levity to the discussion and make it easier to discuss librarian archetypes which are often ill-defined. To make this discussion a little easier to follow, it may help to define some underlying terms.

Library culture

As with Supreme Court Justice Potter Stewart's 1964 definition of hardcore pornography, most people would have a difficult time defining the concept of 'library culture,' yet library staff know it when they see it. For MacDonald and Thomas, library culture is overly-focused on copyright and patron privacy which impedes support of collaborative research communities (2006: 5). For others, library culture can be defined by the Unshelved (*http://www.unshelved .com/*) web-comic which portrays the staff of a public library. The Librarians in the Movies filmography (*http://emp .byui.edu/raishm/films/introduction.html*) gives an overview of how librarians are portrayed in popular culture. For the purposes of this chapter, library culture is the multifaceted relationship between librarians and library staff and users of library materials and services – hereafter called library users.

Alpha geeks

According to the Net Lingo online dictionary, an alpha geek is 'The most knowledgeable, technically proficient person in an office or work group.' The term is normally used in a network administration or computer science context and already has a touch of irony to it. In the library context, alpha geeks are most likely systems librarians who keep vital technology running. The role of alpha geek is based on context, though, and an alpha geek in the reference department might be the librarian most comfortable with new technology.

As technology has become more prevalent and important in library culture, the role of the systems librarian has become more important even if it has not always become more prominent. The role of the alpha geek, however, has become more prominent as technology-dependent library staff turn to the most knowledgeable and accessible person around – an alpha geek – for help with their technology problems.

Luddites

According to the *Encyclopædia Britannica Online*, 'The term Luddite is now used broadly to signify individuals or groups opposed to technological change' (Encyclopædia Britannica Online, 2009). The original Luddites were not strictly against new technology per se. They did react, sometimes violently, to technological changes that hurt their standing or security in society. The Luddite movement in the early 1800s was a reaction against real changes in society and many of the Luddites' worries about the effects of technology were legitimate and, indeed, prophetic.

While the original Luddite movement may have been more nuanced than the modern perception, this chapter focuses on the modern meaning of Luddite.

> Luddism is portrayed as all that is negative, hopeless and deluded. It is unintelligent, probably violent;

indiscriminate and futile; the action of ignorant, backward-looking workers; anachronistic, brutal and destructive, lacking in imagination; opposed to progress. The accusation of 'Luddism' has become a ritual incantation that forecloses debate on the social and political meanings, the causes and effects, of technological change. (Webster, 1986: 2)

Jones (2006: 231) suggests that 'Many people who identify with the term "Luddite" just want to reduce or control the technology that is all around us and to question its utility – to force us not to take technology for the water in which we swim.' Jones (2006: 174–175) also indicates that 'Modern (and now postmodern) technology is routinely understood as an autonomous, disembodied force operating behind any specific application, the effect of a system that is somehow much less material, more ubiquitous, than any mere "machinery".'

Technology marches inexorably on, even in the world of librarianship. Libraries no longer relied on scrolls following the advent of the book. Although library staff may admit to often wanting to kick their computers, anyone working in a modern library must realize that not even the most technophobic library staff could really be considered Luddites. Technology is too critical to libraries for the term Luddite to be anything but a very ironic term. Still, those ironically labeled 'Luddites' in a library setting may not be against technology or change so much as they are worried about the implications of new technologies on library services, professionalism, standards, scholarliness, privacy or other things held important in library culture. That said, changes in library technology and practice over the last 30 years have defined library culture as differentiated between computer power-users and those who keep up with technology out of necessity.

To illustrate this point it might be helpful to think of two opposing camps: alpha geeks vs. Luddites. Both camps share the same environment and have the same goal of accomplishing the library's mission. They may view the world in very different ways, but they need to work together effectively. Keeping in mind that these two opposing camps are extreme caricatures, the alpha geek camp can roughly be described as systems librarians and other technologists while the Luddite camp would encompass librarians and staff, whether they are in public services or behind the scenes, who must use technology to do their jobs but do not, necessarily, embrace it. We've created two librarian archetypes to represent these camps: Annie AlphaGeek and Larry Luddite. These characters represent extremes and do not represent any individual either author knows.

Shift in focus from library processes to services

The original Luddite movement occurred as the Industrial Revolution was shifting the British economy from a rural/ agricultural base to an urban/industrial base. Today, economies in the developed world are similarly shifting from industrial to service economies. The role of libraries continues to shift from primarily being storehouses of information (in print or electronic formats) to being providers of services: access to aggregator databases, expertise in finding and evaluating information, and more. This shift in the role of libraries is, of course, changing the day-to-day work of library employees at all levels of the organization and it is affecting employees in different roles in the library in different ways. One constant, however, is the increasing involvement of the library user in all types of library work.

Reference

The pop culture stereotype of a librarian with a hair-bun shushing library users and making sure every book is back in its place on the shelf is modeled on a reference librarian. An illustrative example is provided by the head librarian in the 1992 movie *The Gun in Betty Lou's Handbag* who believes that the goal of every library book is to be returned to the shelf unmutilated (*The Gun in Betty Lou's Handbag*, 2003). While the stereotype is, of course, overblown, there is a grain of truth in the traditional role of the reference librarian. Far from being happy when all books are back on the shelves in their proper order, most librarians are happier when the collections are being used. Perhaps the grain of truth in the stereotype comes from library culture's emphasis on quality and completeness of information over speed. Among reference and instruction librarians in academia, there is also a debate about whether their primary role is to provide information to the library user or to teach the users to find the information themselves. In the not-so-distant past, reference librarians were called on to know their collections and, in many cases, look up relevant information for library users. As information shifted from print to electronic formats, librarians became the gatekeepers – the experts who knew the most efficient techniques for doing pay-per-search research on systems like Dialog. Information seekers needed to go through librarians to get the information (Goetsch, 2008: 158). As information becomes increasingly electronic, networked and ubiquitous, the role of the reference and instruction librarian is shifting from being gatekeeper to guide.

Information seekers no longer need professional library expertise to find a place to look – Google is everywhere. Library users no longer operate in an information desert but now drown in a sea of web pages, Wikipedia articles, online newspapers and articles in aggregator databases. In many ways, this is a wonderful time to be a librarian and have a world of opportunities. Libraries are making efforts to use technology like electronic resource management (ERM) systems and full-text finders to give more direct access to library users and remove librarians further from their gatekeeper role. In many academic libraries, budget pressures and new technologies are '... making it essential that students, faculty and staff can access these resources without assistance from librarians' (Fuller et al., 2009: 387). Now it is more important for reference and instruction librarians to teach library skills to library users and focus on teaching users to evaluate the quality of what they find.

Access services

Access services departments composed of circulation, course reserves and interlibrary loans are similarly finding their roles increasingly devolving to library users.

> As user-generated renewals and self check-out systems are advancing in library services, the environment remains dynamic. In addition, consortium agreements and access to member library catalogs with holdings information blur the lines between reference and access services. (Su, 2008: 78)

Interlibrary loan systems such as Illiad now allow library users to start their own requests for books and articles from other libraries. The OCLC system, formerly the secret weapon of

ILL librarians, has morphed into *http://worldcat.org*, where information seekers can search across several library catalogs for books in their area and, at times, bypass ILL altogether. More advanced circulation systems are allowing library users to place books on hold or request delivery of books and articles through the library catalog. Library users can check their circulation records, pay fines and, of course, complain, all through sophisticated circulation systems. As e-books and online articles become more widespread and accessible, even course reserves systems are becoming a more user-oriented library function as instructors use persistent URLs to link their students to online readings in course management systems.

Technical services

Technical services departments are experiencing shifts in what they do, day-to-day, along with significant shifts in the resources used to accomplish their tasks. Technical services staff increasingly struggle with providing bibliographic control to electronic resources, e-books, and even relocated print materials as space shortages define availability. Technology assists in providing control through data-loads and exporting data to various vendors and consortia; electronic templates organize incoming work. New metadata standards like Dublin Core and METS require additional staff education. Shelf Ready processing reduces the impact that staff has in preparing books for shelving. Budget cuts and outsourcing often result in reductions in technical services staff.

Systems

In addition to changes to the above cultural groups (reference, access services, technical services) the role of systems librarian is also changing. For several decades the systems librarian has focused on technology. Heid (2007, para. 1) indicates that:

> IT people and library people have not been inclined to come to the concept of service with the same view. For IT, it's been all about keeping the servers and systems up, the websites going, and the help desk calls and their turnaround times to a minimum. For library professionals, service has meant keeping multimedia information and reference accessible; books, tapes, CDs, and other sources in order; and the environment primed for research and study.

Systems librarians can even on occasion create the very systems that users and peers request. Systems librarians at many universities, for example, spearheaded the integration of SFX into their institution's research databases.

In recent years systems librarians have begun to develop a more public role from the previous wizard behind the curtain who magically made things happen.

History of library information technology

Evolution of technology in libraries

Advances in technology in both the culture at large and within libraries have defined library staff positions and the services offered by libraries. Before the advent of computers, the availability of typewriters defined many tasks performed in libraries. In previous centuries, the quill pen was a great breakthrough to aid in the accuracy and the speed of library work.

But this digression does not lead us forward. In the 1960s computers began to have an impact on libraries and by 1967, with the advent of OCLC and other large bibliographic utilities, 'systems librarian' began to emerge as a job classification in libraries. Library systems work involved working with remote host computers, interacting with computer vendors, and scrambling to keep up with the changing technology. In the early years of library computing, separately hosted services were available to assist with reference, collection building and acquisitions, circulation and cataloging with the eventual creation of an online catalog. Available automated systems did not talk to one another. Library employees began to compete for systems positions which would have an impact in this new realm of library work. Some library staff preferred to distance themselves from this new technology and instead attempted to maintain the status quo (pre-computer), following historical patterns of service and preferring printed resources rather than information available through a computer.

It's the 1970s. Annie AlphaGeek spends late night hours trying to learn about OCLC while struggling with CLSI configuration tables during the day. Larry Luddite successfully hides from training and refuses to serve on task forces to define system options. He often complains to colleagues about problems with the systems, pointing out reduced service and increased complexity.

Systems librarian as hardware guru

When computers were introduced into libraries, the systems staff learned the technology 'on the fly.' Systems staff became conversant with DOS and later Pascal and still later C. The systems librarian learned network and hardware details. Lavagnino (1997: 218, 220) indicates:

> The systems librarian ... was concerned with mainframe and minicomputer systems development and implementation, and usually was found working for bibliographic utilities, vendors, or large university libraries developing in-house systems. The systems generally were developed to handle functions used by staff, such as circulation or acquisitions; few public services functions were automated. These systems librarians dealt mostly with technical issues such as setting terminal characteristics, managing appropriate inputs and outputs to and from the system, running indexing jobs, and backing up the system. This involved interacting with programmers in developing the system and with technicians in keeping it running, and sometimes in operating the system and training library staff. These early systems librarians did not interact with the public, the college or university students, staff, and faculty but instead were limited to working with library and computer center staff and faculty.

As libraries (and the culture at large) became more and more dependent on technology, the geeks and hardware gurus held the power to aid library staff charged with maintaining the day-to-day workflow of the libraries. Frequently the technical staff began to talk a special techno-speak while the general library staff believed that these technicians no longer knew how to speak English. Often the library staff became distrustful of the systems librarians. Several articles highlight this tension between library staff and library technologists including Davidson and Rusk

(1996: 302–5), reporting that differences in underlying values and styles of librarians and technologists created difficulties in reaching consensus.

> It's 1975. Annie AlphaGeek is the lady with the magic fingers. She can fix barcode scanners and test new network connections, while assisting the staff with their problems. Larry Luddite is able to continue to avoid most library technology and when required to use the circulation system he is so inept that he is not asked to assist with this work again.

Era of the personal computer

The era of the personal computer began in 1976 with the invention of the Apple computer by Steve Jobs and Steve Wozniak. By the 1980s the personal computer was revolutionizing the culture, and libraries were quick to join the revolution. Word processing, spreadsheets and databases were creating a high-efficiency workforce. Library employees were dependent on the special skills of the systems librarians. Many general library staff saw systems librarians as critical to their work. Yet some staff continued to be distrustful or unnecessarily demanding of technical staff.

> It's 1980. Annie AlphaGeek has become exceptionally efficient at completing her demanding assignments using her top-of-the-line workstation. She emails vendors and colleagues all over the country to keep her various

systems working smoothly. Larry Luddite has a personal computer but avoids using it for all but very routine tasks. Whenever possible Larry complains that the Systems Office is inept and unable to support library staff when they have problems.

Integrated Library Systems

In the 1970s and early 1980s Integrated Library Systems began to appear. During the implementation of these large, comprehensive library management systems the systems librarian had a great deal of power, if not necessarily in-depth knowledge and technical training. The systems librarian often had responsibility for virtually all aspects of library processing including cataloging, acquisitions and circulation. Library services such as reference and inter-library loan were very dependent upon tools created or managed by the Systems Office. Webster (1986: 149) states '... the online librarian currently receives much status from users who are dependent upon his or her expertise as the gatekeeper of the system.'

It's 1990. Larry Luddite spends most of his workday on a computer connected to the ILS. He knows what he needs to know to do his job, but gets upset with changes to the software and panics when the system goes down. Annie AlphaGeek gets very frustrated with Larry since most of the library staff are flexible and understand that the system is always changing.

Library culture mirrors the culture at large

Over time the technology advanced to incorporate the internet, networking within the organization and beyond to the far reaches of the globe. Libraries kept pace as print resources were converted to online versions. Online instruction and distance learning became commonplace. Email became a standard for both professional and personal communication. In the late 1990s Google launched a suite of online services which continues to expand. Social computing through Facebook, YouTube, Twitter, PDAs and similar software allows the computer to become an extension of the individual. Melchionda (2007: 125) adds:

> No one can deny the huge explosion of the internet, which has carried with it many contradictions – since the growth of networked technologies in libraries, there has always been a segment of library professionals expressing care – and sometimes fear – for the future of the profession, not to mention those traditionalists who almost despised the huge presence of internet-related technologies. Some were critical toward the internet because of its chaos, its lack of structure and of knowledge organization. Others were worried about the independence acquired by users, who are encouraged to access freely and use collections and electronic shelves and services without librarians' intervention.

It's 2000. Larry Luddite has joined the online community and relies on multiple computer systems to do his job and to have some fun when he's not working. He's continually asking the Systems Office questions about computing at work as well as at home. Annie AlphaGeek is feeling a new kind of strain as public services librarians and library users increasingly use social networking sites like Twitter, Facebook, Del.Icio.Us and others to share information and push the boundaries of library technology. Increasingly, she feels overwhelmed at the number of new technologies to keep up with but happy that the flexibility and creativity she learned over the last 30 years allows her to keep up. She's looking forward to the new ways that technology will allow people to use information more effectively.

Role of the systems librarian

Systems staff have counterparts outside the library

Many positions in libraries are unique to libraries: bookstack supervisors, interlibrary loan coordinators and reference manager librarians. The role of systems librarian often integrates tasks and responsibilities from non-library system departments such as database manager, application programmer, desktop support, system administration and network manager. A systems librarian must have knowledge and experience of libraries, but the critical component of the job is systems. A systems librarian must install, upgrade and troubleshoot both hardware and software. The systems librarian must often train library staff in the various technical tools acquired by the library.

Changes in technology have defined the systems librarian

As technical library tools have advanced and as technology within the culture has evolved, the role of systems librarian has been stretched. Software to maintain security in the network and on workstations has become increasingly important in an environment of rampant computer fraud and abuse. Support for digital collections, electronic books, and online databases requires new expertise. Systems librarians find themselves supporting laptops, PDAs, faxes, camcorders, elaborate scanning equipment and high-end network printers. Software functionality continues to change; mobile applications become more important as many library users rely on PDAs for information. The library catalog evolves with new discovery tools and emerging software. The cost of hardware and storage regularly decreases, resulting in the diversification of available technological tools and the creation of serious support issues for the systems librarian. Online problem reporting tools have become sophisticated and management tools have become more effective.

Changes in the needs of users have affected the role of systems librarians

More than in earlier decades, the needs of library users are shaping the role of systems librarians. Users want materials and services *now*. Users expect a broad range of technical support including customized printing, fax and scanning. They want searching to be not only intuitive but automatic. Document delivery allows faculty and students access without entering the library. Relevance ranking, as with Google, places the system in the position of identifying the best resources. Library users expect the computer to pull disparate but related resources together with link-resolvers like Ex Libris' SFX or EBSCO's LinkSource. Recommender services connect library users to other library users who have opinions about resources.

How does the systems librarian fit into the maze of requests and demands? Frequently the needs of library users are not the same as those of library staff, who are hoping for support in doing their day-to-day tasks in the most efficient, automated way possible. Increasingly library administrators are saying that if the library does not offer a service that the users want, then the users will just find other non-library vendors, like Google or Amazon, to meet their needs.

Communication between general librarians and systems librarians

If alpha geeks and Luddites form two separate tribes who work in the same library environment, it is clear that they will have to learn to communicate and work effectively with one another. Indeed, as technology becomes more ubiquitous and new technologies increasingly bring systems librarians into closer contact with other library staff and library users, the interpersonal communication skills of both alpha geeks and Luddites will become correspondingly important.

Personality

There is little doubt that different personality types are drawn to different professions, even within the sphere of library culture. Williamson et al. found in their 2008 study that:

... high extraversion, low tough-mindedness, and high teamwork (among other variables for the various clusters) characterized person-oriented academic reference librarians, special librarians, public librarians, school librarians, distance education librarians and records managers. For the technique-oriented specialties operational work style and low customer service orientation characterized catalogers, and high assertiveness and high tough-mindedness characterized the archivists and systems librarians. (Williamson et al., 2008 pp. 282–283)

High assertiveness and tough-mindedness are not typical characteristics that foster effective communication and collaborative work styles. Systems librarians will need to develop more inclusive communication styles in order to be a part of effective library-wide technological developments.

Channels of communication

An informal poll of systems librarians at six institutions was conducted by the authors. Responses revealed no clear consensus on the best methods for systems librarians and other librarians to communicate effectively. All respondents agreed that formal methods of communication, including a problem-reporting structure, were of paramount importance. Structured communication allows for information to be standardized, tracked and monitored. There was reduced consensus on the benefits of informal or casual communication. The fear that informal channels of communication might lead to disorganization, extra work or favoritism is balanced by recognition that informal lines of communication promote new ideas, partnerships and progress. Systems librarians should, at least occasionally, forego efficiency in order to utilize more informal methods of communication, thus fostering partnership and creativity.

Communication is, of course, a two-way street, and informal and formal channels of communication have costs and benefits for Luddites, too. Formal channels of communication, like problem-reporting forms or email announcements from the IT department, aid technologists by systematizing information and ensuring that there is enough detailed information for troubleshooting. Unfortunately, formal communication channels presume a basic level of knowledge on the part of the non-technologists. Problem-reporting forms, for example, are only effective if the person filling out the form knows enough about the problem to use the right form or give accurate information. Informal communication, while running the risk of inefficiency, at least allows the Luddite to explain problems and answer questions.

Language itself is often a barrier in technical communication between Luddites and alpha geeks. Leaving aside the issue of jargon, which might make up a chapter on its own, even relatively straightforward terms may have nuances or differences in meaning between technologists and library staff, potentially causing confusion. A podcast, for example, might mean that thing you watch on your computer to a Luddite, while an alpha geek knows that it is an RSS-based serialized set of things to watch on your computer.

Core competency

Many libraries have developed core competency standards which define the level of technical competency for non-technical staff. Training programs often accompany the establishment of a core competency program. One significant advantage of core competency training is the establishment of a common vocabulary and a common understanding of technical processes between the general library staff and the systems librarian. For example, learning to determine the domain in which an application resides or how various removable storage devices work provides a common base from which technical staff and general staff can discuss problems.

Planning and goal setting

Annual or periodic goal setting offers many opportunities for communication between systems librarians and units or subgroups and also between individuals. Often formal systems for gathering input on goals are in place, but periodic *ad hoc* reviews allow library staff to offer opinions while new system developments are in process. In the authors' poll, one participant indicated that people at all levels of the organization can make their requests known to the dean through the proper channels of departmental hierarchy. Additionally work groups, when used effectively, can make suggestions during the design of systems. Many organizations also provide opportunities for everyone to make suggestions during the goal planning process, typically through departmental channels.

Technical tools

Many staff, both systems librarians and general librarians, are shifting their communication to new technologies. Through an informal survey of systems librarians, wikis have been determined to be marginally effective communication tools. Instant messaging exchanges were identified as effective and efficient in responding to the immediate call for help. Intranets allow more complex communication to a large audience of staff or departments by allowing the posting of documentation, special notices or other more extensive communication.

Conclusion

This chapter has highlighted the history of library information technology, utilizing Annie AlphaGeek and Larry Luddite to illustrate the transitions in communication as well as the technology. Library culture is a microcosm of society at large, and, as in the larger society, people are rarely cleanly divided into two distinct and opposing camps. Most systems librarians do not see all new technology as an inherent good and most Luddites in libraries accept the benefits of many new technologies.

The role of the systems librarian has changed over time but has particularly been influenced by the new technologies which have become popular with library users. The systems librarian works within a grid of reference librarians, technical services librarians, access services staff and others. Each staff member experiences shifts in their profession and the resources with which they work. The systems librarian must refine communication skills and must work to understand the issues confronting the general library staff in order to successfully meet the technological needs of the library.

In discussing collaborations between librarians and information technologists, Lippincott indicates that each individual needs to emphasize '... the complementary expertise that each member of the team brings, the need for open and easy communication, the opportunities for mutual teaching and learning, and the development of trust and respect' (Lippincott, 1998: 438). Communication within a context of trust and respect can bridge many differences.

Communication and computer technology have evolved during the last several decades, and those changes have both driven and been driven by changes in our society and culture. It is tempting to say that the one thing that has not changed is change itself, but that cliché overlooks several factors that the authors believe libraries and librarians hold as guiding principles. Regardless of the technologies used or the information sought, librarians' guiding principle has been and remains helping people find the relevant information they need. Regardless of which tribe they belong to, Luddite and alpha geek librarians work together to make library materials available to library users. The emergence of social media has accelerated a trend of making library users more directly involved in using library resources and finding their own information and has, as a result, changed the day-to-day jobs of all types of library staff, including systems librarians. Whether an alpha geek, a Luddite, or somewhere in between, librarians adapt to changing circumstances and the changing needs of library users through effective communication and by maintaining a healthy sense of humor.

References

Davidson, J., and Rusk, C. (1996). Creating a university Web in a team environment. *Journal of Academic Librarianship, 22*(4), 302. doi:10.1016/S0099–1333(96)90123–8.

Encyclopædia Britannica Online. (2009). *Luddite.* Retrieved May 6, 2010 from *http://www.britannica.com/EBchecked/topic/350725/Luddite*

Fuller, K., Livingston, J., Brown, S. W., Cowan, S., Wood, T., and Porter, L. (2009). Making unmediated access to e-resources a reality. *Reference & User Services Quarterly, 48*(3), 287–301.

Goetsch, L. A. (2008). Reinventing our work: New and emerging roles for academic librarians. *Journal of Library Administration, 48*(2), 157–172. doi:10.1080/01930820802231351

The gun in Betty Lou's handbag. Moyle, A., (Director), Bickley, G. C., (Writer) and Kroopf, S., (Producer). (2003). [Video/DVD] Burbank, CA: Touchstone Home Video.

Heid, S. (06/01/2007). *Culture morph.* Retrieved May 6, 2010 from *http://campustechnology.com/articles/2007/06/culture-morph.aspx*

Jones, S. E. (2006). *Against technology: from the Luddites to Neo-Luddism.* New York: Routledge.

Lavagnino, M. (1997). Networking and the role of the academic systems librarian: An evolutionary perspective. *College and Research Libraries, 58*(3), 217.

Lippincott, J. (1998). Working together: building collaboration between librarians and information technologists. *Information Technology and Libraries, 17*(2), 83.

MacDonald, R. H., and Thomas, C. (2006). Disconnects between library culture and millennial generation values. *EDUCAUSE Quarterly, 29*(4), October 22, 2009–4–6. Retrieved May 6, 2010 from *http://net.educause.edu/ir/library/pdf/EQM0640.pdf*

Melchionda, M. (2007). Librarians in the age of the internet: their attitudes and roles. *New Library World, 108*(3/4), 123–40. doi:10.1108/03074800710735339

NetLingo.*Alpha Geek.* Retrieved December 2, 2009, from *http://www.netlingo.com/word/alpha-geek.php*

Su, M. (2008). Beyond circulation: The evolution of access services and its relationship to reference librarianship. *Reference Librarian, 49*(1), 77–86. doi:10.1080/02763870802103795

Webster, F. (1986). In Robins, K. (Ed.), *Information technology: A Luddite analysis.* Norwood, N.J.: Ablex Pub. Corp.

Williamson, J. M., Pemberton, A. E. and Lounsbury, J. W. (2008). Personality traits of individuals in different specialties of librarianship. *Journal of Documentation, 64*(2), 273. doi:10.1108/00220410810858056

The Current Environment

5

The status of the field

Edward Iglesias

Previous research

Research in this field proved somewhat limited. The vast majority of studies focus on the field of librarianship in general.[1] The single best overview of the field until this point has to be the one dedicated to the subject by *Library Hi Tech*.[2] Although this source is quite dated it is valuable in seeing how much the field has changed in recent years. The article 'From library systems to mainstream software: how Web technologies are changing the role of the systems librarian' gives a very good overview of changes that at that point were just beginning but are now the norm. Still other areas have not changed at all, such as the importance of linking and stability or the growing importance of XML.

Other areas that have remained relatively unchanged are public expectations. The rapid increase in mainstream technological advancements raises expectations from our library system users. Increasing familiarity with commercial features on the Web, such as the online shopping cart or rail ticket booking systems, creates a high level of user anticipation. As students increasingly pay for library services, either directly or indirectly, facilities such as online request forms or subject resource listings are considered essential developments of the library system. In systems terms, these may require advanced testing and configuration (Guinea, 2003).

The other trademark volume that people turn to when trying to figure out what systems librarians do is *The Accidental Systems Librarian* by Rachel Singer Gordon. The work still provides the new systems librarian with good advice although the specific software suggested is very dated, as would be expected from a book written in 2003.

The book *CORE Technology Competencies for Librarians & Library Staff: A LITA Guide* (Thompson, 2008; Lodwick, 2010) published by the Library Information and Technology Association addresses many of these issues in Susan M. Thompson's chapter 'Management and Technology Competencies for the Systems Librarian.' Her broad overview of the field is an excellent starting point. Especially valuable are her discussion of the research of Lavagnino and its updating by Ross and Marion about the stages of development of the systems librarian (Thompson, 2010: 76–7). Lavagnino argues that there is a systemic and evolutionary growth in the role of the systems librarian that is marked in stages where 'One' marks a time before systems librarians and 'Four' begins in the 1990s with the growth of systems staff and distributed computing coming to the forefront (Lavagnino, 1997: 219). Ross and Marion propose a Stage Five:

> The transition from Stage Four to Stage Five is occurring. Some of the characteristics that marked the arrival of Stage Four have grown at such a tremendous rate and affected systems librarianship to such a degree that they can be identified as major components in the push to Stage Five. Among these are standards, client/server

architecture, and support for our patrons. (Ross & Marmion, 2000: 5)

This research certainly seems to agree with the findings in this book as will be seen in further chapters.

Otherwise much research has been focused on the applications that systems librarians work with rather than their environment.[3] This volume hopes to address these through a compilation of research from around the world. To begin with, below are the results of a short survey on the subject which was meant to be a snapshot of systems librarians' environment as of 2009.

Who we are

The systems librarian plays a unique role in libraries. From the earliest incarnations there has never been a set job description. For the purposes of the survey the criterion was: 'You are the one who has to fix the ILS (Integrated Library System) if it breaks.' This carries certain assumptions. First, that there is an ILS. While certainly every academic and public library of any size has an Integrated Library System there are many small libraries such as special libraries and law libraries that do not. Additionally, some respondents were employed by consortia that host the library's ILS for them even though they are not in the library themselves.

Overall the picture of systems librarians is one of a very diverse group, often in transition. Many of the job titles such as 'Director of Library Services, formerly Manager, Library Systems and Technical Services' illustrated this. The variety of departments that systems librarians are a part of is also quite diverse. This group responded to an email sent out to the email lists LITA-L, Code4Lib and the IUG Innopac List. A total of 205 respondents answered questions ranging from job title to an estimate of time spent with vendors.[4] As stated above, the only requirement for being a 'Systems Librarian' for the purposes of this survey was responsibility for the maintenance of an ILS. Below is a summary of those findings.

The survey

The first question asked was 'What is your title?' This question is important if one is to make sense of the system librarian's status in the workplace.

Q1 What is your title?

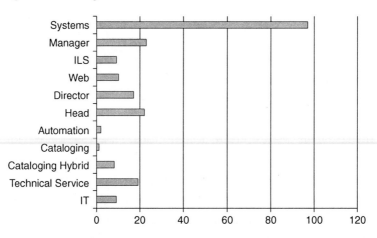

The labels in the chart are very rough categories and refer to the number of times a word appeared in a title rather than the title itself. Careful readers may note that these numbers add up to 217 rather than 205. This was due to a certain amount of overlap in titles. A 'Library Systems Manager' might count in both 'Systems' and 'Manager.' The criterion was whether the words 'systems' or 'manager' were used. All disclaimers aside, it is clear that the word 'systems' is still the most prevalent way to describe the person responsible for the maintenance of the ILS. The terms Cataloger and Automation Librarian were the least prevalent, even including the Cataloger Hybrid category which encompassed titles like 'Cataloger/Web Services Specialist'. Of some interest is the prevalence of the term Manager. Most systems librarians seem to manage people as well as things. This will be revisited in question 10. It does not appear that this confusion is limited to the library world. The O*Net Occupational Information Network only lists a category for 'Librarians'.[5]

The next question was 'Do you work for IT or for the library?' This gets to one of the biggest trends in academic libraries where the information technology department is given control of the library's management of information resources. This often extends to the direct supervision of the systems librarian. In the survey pool a full 87 percent of the respondents still work for the library exclusively.

Q2 Do you work for IT or for the library?

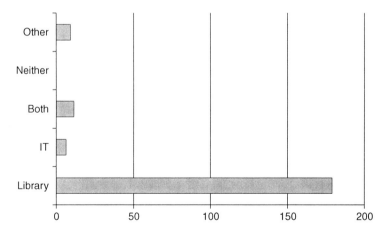

However, several respondents indicated they found the distinction artificial, such as when working in consortia for libraries but not in part of any one library. There were also cases where IT was a department within the library. Information technology as a department made a stronger showing when dealing with hardware in general. The field is split between those who take care of public computers in-house and those who outsource to IT.

Q3 Who maintains your public computers?

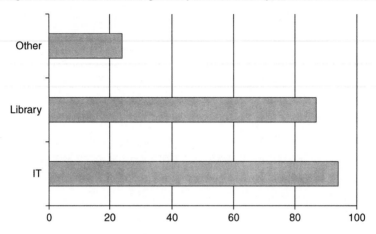

This trend diverges a bit with 52 percent of respondents reporting that the library maintains staff computers and nearly all 81 percent reporting that IT is responsible for the maintenance of network hardware. IT tends to handle printing solutions about 52 percent of the time while the web server is in the library's hands 50 percent of the time. Predictably, the library handles the administration of the web server 50 percent of the time as well. As for what departments are called this was obviously a sensitive subject for some who were quick to respond with responses such as:

> no name, just a systems librarian. Is talk of 'technical services' but would need staff.

Below is another keyword chart listing the most common phrases used to describe departments.

Q10 What is the name of your department?

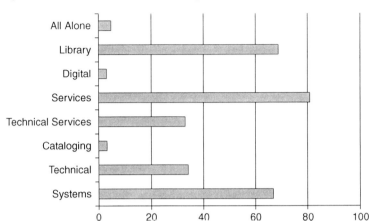

Despite the solitary nature of some respondents the vast majority are independent departments.

Q11 Are you part of technical services, public services, an independent department within the library, or IT?

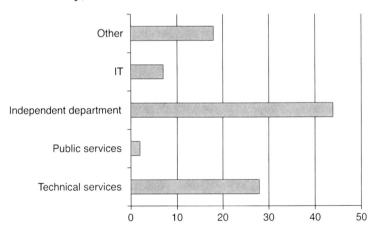

The respondents also held an MLS or equivalent by a vast majority (85 percent) and also supervised staff 58 percent of the time. All told 81 percent supervised one or more staff.

The question of whether the systems track was chosen was of particular interest to the author. The aforementioned *Accidental Systems Librarian* by Rachel Singer Gordon is a classic because so many systems librarians feel unprepared for their responsibilities. In recent years library schools have started offering 'systems tracks' which offer some greater degree of preparation to the new candidate. Our respondents did not take advantage of this sort of education, with 82 percent saying they had not taken these classes and had learned on the job.

Another area where there is perhaps insufficient training is that of dealing with library vendors: 63 percent reported that more than 5 percent of their time is spent dealing with vendors. This is starting to move in the direction of contract and project management more than anything technological. As libraries continue to move, towards outsourcing services systems librarians will increasingly be in this transitional state where they must continue to manage legacy systems while increasingly dealing with vendors. Even if many libraries decide to deploy open source options the vast majority will not have the staff or budget to handle complex customizations themselves. These complex tasks will be outsourced to vendors or technical consortia who have the expertise to deal with complicated programming projects.

Conclusion

The overall survey indicates a few trends. First, the library environment is conservative enough that even though realities change (nature of work, required qualifications, etc. ...), libraries have been generally slow to reflect this in new job titles, job descriptions and training opportunities. There also seems to be an increased sense of frustration as staff are often expected to be the 'technical experts' no matter what that technology may be. While major ILS vendors all provide training in their products many of the new technologies, especially those that are open source, do not have a clear path to attaining mastery. As libraries transform themselves they would be wise to listen to the words of David W. Lewis, Dean of the Library at IUPUI University. His work, 'A Strategy for Academic Libraries in the First Quarter of the 21st Century ...', focuses on the changes that need to occur in academic libraries, starting with four assumptions:

- Libraries are the mechanism for providing the subsidy that is required if information is to be used efficiently in communities and organizations.

- Libraries confront a variety of disruptive technologies and these technologies will disrupt libraries.

- Real change requires real change. Incremental adjustments at the margins will not be sufficient.

- We have a window of opportunity. Books and libraries are revered in academic culture and librarians in general are well thought of by faculty and even administrators.[6]

The first three assumptions seem to be backed up by responses in this study and are obviously strongly felt in the systems world. Libraries must continue to embrace change or face irrelevance. In order to accommodate that change, staff face some challenges. It is no longer sufficient to expect technology to be the sole province of some other department. Indeed, many of the changes that are most visible in libraries are the result of reference librarians using unsupported tools to meet users where they are. As systems continue to grow in complexity the choice will be between hiring staff who are able and willing to take on these challenges, or to close. Future budgets will not allow for staff who are averse to technology and change. Paradoxically, as staff become more technologically competent the role of the systems librarian is likely to become one where there is an increased focus on enterprise level solutions and contract management as well as coordination of resources. The future looks bright as long as change is embraced. It is not that systems librarians are losing their role as technology specialists, but that they are increasingly becoming technology coordinators who must look at staff as peer specialists who probably know more about a particular technology than they do. It is only through a team approach of distributed expertise that libraries as organizations can hope not only to keep up, but to lead.

Appendix

Survey questions

1. What is your title?

2. Do you work for IT or for the library?
   Library
   IT
   Both
   Neither

3. Who maintains your public computers?
   IT
   Library

4. Who maintains your faculty/staff computers in the library?
   IT
   Library

5. Who maintains your network hardware (routers, NAS, etc.)?
   IT
   Library

6. Who maintains your printing solution (aka Pharos)?
   IT
   Library

7. Who hosts your webserver?
   IT
   Library
   Other

8. Who is in charge of systems administration on your webserver?
   IT
   Library
   Other

9. Where is your ILS housed?
   Library
   IT Datacenter
   Other

10. What is the name of your department?

11. Are you part of:
    Technical Services
    Public Services
    An independent department within the library
    IT

12. Do you have an ALA accredited MLS or equivalent?

13. Do you supervise employees?

14. If so how many?
    1
    1–3

3–5

>5

15. Did you do the 'systems track' in library school?

16. Estimate how much of your time you spend dealing with vendors.

<5%

5%

>5%

Table of responses

IT or Library	Response total	Response percent
Library	179	87%
IT	6	3%
Both	11	5%
Neither	0	0%
Other	9	4%
Maintains public computers		
IT	94	46%
Library	87	42%
Other	24	12%
Faculty/staff computers		
IT	72	35%
Library	107	52%
Other	26	13%
Network		
IT	167	81%
Library	24	12%
Other	14	7%
Printing		
IT	107	52%
Library	64	31%
Other	34	17%
Webserver		
IT	102	50%
Library	76	37%
Other	27	13%

Sysadmin		
IT	76	37%
Library	103	50%
Other	26	13%
ILS		
IT	85	41%
Library	87	42%
Vendor Hosted	11	5%
Other	22	11%
Organization		
Technical Services	57	28%
Public Services	5	2%
Independent Dept	91	44%
IT	15	7%
Other	37	18%
MLS		
Yes	174	85%
No	31	15%
Supervise		
Yes	118	58%
No	87	42%
How Many		
1	23	19%
1–3	49	41%
3–5	23	19%
>5	25	21%
Systems Track		
Yes	36	18%
No	169	82%
Vendors		
<5%	75	37%
5%–10%	85	41%
>10%	45	22%

Notes

1. See for example Applegate (2009) or Steele (2009).
2. *Library Hi Tech*, Volume 21, Number 3 (September 17, 2003).
3. See for example Featherstone & Wang, 2009.

4. A full list of the questions and responses is available in the appendix.
5. The listing is at *http://www.occupationalinfo.org/onet/31502a.html* (accessed May 6, 2010).
6. Quoted in 'Exploring Models For Academic Libraries'; for full article see Lewis, 2007.

Works cited

Applegate, Rachel. 'Who Benefits? Unionization and Academic Libraries and Librarians.' *Library Quarterly* 79.4 (2009): 443–63. Print.

'Exploring Models For Academic Libraries.' *http://acrlblog.org/2007/03/12/exploring-models-for-academic-libraries.* Web. 22 Feb. 2010.

Featherstone, Robin, and Lei Wang. 'Enhancing Subject Access to Electronic Collections with VuFind.' *Journal of Electronic Resources in Medical Libraries* 6.4 (2009): 294–306. Web.

Gordon, Rachel Singer. *The Accidental Systems Librarian.* Medford, N.J.: Information Today, Inc. (2003). Print.

Guinea, Janet. 'Building bridges: the role of the systems librarian in a university library.' *Library Hi Tech* 21.3 (2003): 325–32. Print.

Lavagnino, Merri Beth. 'Networking and the Role of the Academic Systems Librarian: An Evolutionary Perspective.' *College & Research Libraries* 58.3 (1997): 217–31. Print.

Lewis, David W. 'A Strategy for Academic Libraries in the First Quarter of the 21st Century.' *College & Research Libraries* 68.5 (2007): 418–34. Web.

Lodwick, David. 'Core technology competencies for librarians and library staff: a LITA guide.' *Technical Services Quarterly* 27.1 (2010): 136–7. Web.

Rhyno, Arthur. 'From library systems to mainstream software: how Web technologies are changing the role of the systems librarian.' *Library Hi Tech* 21.3 (2003): 289–96. Print.

Ross, Mary and Dan Marmion. 'Systems librarians and the client/server environment.' *Library Hi Tech* 18.2 (2000): 151–7. Print.

Steele, Anitra. 'Flying with the phoenixes: avoiding job burnout as a librarian and a manager.' *Children & Libraries: The Journal of the Association for Library Service to Children* 7.3 (2009): 51–52. Web.

Thompson, Susan M. *Core Technology Competencies for Librarians and Library Staff: A LITA Guide.* 1st edn. Neal-Schuman Publishers, 2008. Print.

6

Building winning partnerships with vendors

Huibin (Heather) Cai

Understanding the vendor's business

Depending on the nature of your job, you may deal with more or only a few vendors. For example, if you manage electronic resources, you may deal with a number of database vendors simultaneously; if you maintain an Integrated Library System (ILS), you may deal with an ILS vendor most of the time. Knowing a vendor's business puts you in a more relevant position when you face a vendor-related issue.

Understanding the vendor's business has a significant importance in selecting an ILS system, as you will be working with your chosen system for many years. The past and the future of the company, the quality of their service, the functionality and usability of the product, the flexibility and extensibility of the system, the interoperability with existing systems, etc., all should be taken into consideration. The whole process of selecting an ILS system is very complicated, which will not be discussed in this chapter. In fact, in many cases you don't really have the choice to select an ILS system – when you accept an offer of a systems librarian's position, you also agree to work with the ILS system that was chosen for you as well as the vendor that supports the system. To that end, understanding the vendor's business perhaps should really start from your job-hunting phase.

There is no need to know everything for every vendor you deal with. You can selectively expand your knowledge more on some vendors than others according to their importance to your job. Getting information about your vendors is made much easier nowadays than before. You can visit the vendor's web site, which usually contains a wealth of information about the company, products, solutions and contact information, etc. You can subscribe to the vendor's blog or Twitter page for the latest updates. You can join the vendor's email discussion lists, attend user conferences and workshops, and check out the vendor exhibits, etc. to enrich your vendor knowledge. Library Technology Guides (*http://www.librarytechnology.org*), maintained by Marshall Breeding, is a great source for library vendor information as well as for library technology in general. Your professional network may offer you additional insight into vendor business.

Below is a list of some major aspects of vendor business that you should know about:

- *Fundamental changes*: Business model changes and strategic initiatives can have a great impact on library operations and services and may influence the future of libraries. Although such fundamental changes normally do not happen overnight, you still need to maintain sensitivity, observe the progress, and be proactive to the changes.

- *Product lines*: As long as a product is still in its life cycle, the vendor will regularly update it and constantly release new versions. A product update usually contains new features, enhancements, or improvements that you should be aware of. A new version usually implies architectural changes that deserve intensive attention. It is important to know how long a current version will be supported so that you can plan for an upgrade. This piece of information usually comes with the new version's release notes. New products may be even more interesting to you as they address new issues and problems that face the library world.

- *Services*: Vendors may be more flexible than you thought in providing services. Some common service types may include technical support, on-site training, software installation, outsourcing and hosted service, etc. Knowing what business options are available to you allows you to make informed decisions. Discuss your special needs with your vendors; together you may work something out. Quality of service is another important factor; for example, what service level they support and how promptly they respond to customer inquiries and questions.

- *Workflows and procedures*: Any company that has run a business for some time should have certain workflows and procedures in place for certain types of business. For instance, an ILS vendor may focus on workflows and procedures for system upgrades, regular updates, service packs and system patches. The workflows and procedures are a mechanism for quality assurance. Knowing how things are handled at the vendor side enables effective communication with the vendor.

- *Research and development*: Vendors invest in research and development in areas they see as promising. Following up on their important developments may not be enough; try to gain an understanding of their philosophy and methodology.

- *Expertise*: By default, no one knows better about a product than the vendor. In general, vendors are experts in specialized areas. Appreciating their expertise allows you to make best use of their knowledge and skills when needed.

Understanding a vendor's business may take some time but the effort will be worthwhile. You may find your knowledge of the vendor will come in handy sometimes; for example, when you have to negotiate with a vendor, you may feel more confident if you know a lot about them.

Respect

A cordial relationship is built on mutual respect. Some basic rules may apply in vendor relations:

Rule 1: Do your homework before asking questions. Always check vendor documentation first before asking questions in the event that your problem is a common issue. Be resourceful and look for solutions before approaching the vendor.

Rule 2: Respect the vendor's knowledge and expertise. Vendors are not necessarily smarter than their customers, but in general they know more about their products. More often than not, you have to rely on their directions, especially when you encounter a painful or rare issue. Vendors are your extended brain.

Rule 3: Push vendors in a positive way. Due to various reasons, your requests may not be responded to quickly enough. Sometimes, a fix or an enhancement may take months or even years to come through. Complaining could make things worse. Try to make constructive suggestions instead.

Rule 4: Be compliant with internet etiquettes. Your communication with vendors is most likely via the Internet. Be polite and professional in writing and respond in a timely fashion.

Communication

A systems librarian is a bridge person between the library and the vendors. On a constant basis, systems librarians communicate with vendors on various technical issues. The goal of such communication is getting the required results; for example, seeking a technical solution, negotiating a license agreement, or setting up a product demo. To accomplish the goal, a systems librarian must be an effective communicator.

Communication is two-way. Be a good listener. Always make sure you understand the situation on the other side. Ask for clarification whenever needed. Keep the line of communication open even in a difficult situation. Express yourself directly and clearly. For example, when you report a problem, describe it clearly and indicate where the vendor should be looking in diagnosing the problem, and include the exact error message which you or the user sees.

The ideal method of communication would be through a face-to-face meeting, but this may be difficult to arrange if you and your vendor are located in two different places. You could, though, arrange a face-to-face meeting at a conference if you know your vendor is going to participate, too.

Email is a convenient and cost-effective communication tool. Most of the time, you communicate with vendors via email, regardless of geographical location. Email can be used for almost any occasion: general inquiries, questions, requests or discussions, etc.

A CRM (Customer Relationship Management) system, or the like, is a ticket-tracking system, or a communication platform between a vendor and its customers. Vendors use it to keep track of questions received from customers, while customers use it to create, update and check the status of support incidents. CRM is a useful tool for problem reporting, process documenting and knowledge sharing.

Note that neither email nor CRM is a synchronous communication method: there is an expected delay in response. In an emergency situation, you may instead want to use the telephone to draw immediate attention and to get instant support from your vendor. In fact, a telephone conversation usually conveys much richer information, and thus helps the other side understand the scenario more easily and quickly. Use the telephone wisely.

A conference call is a variation of telephone communication, often used in discussion and decision-making processes in a vendor–library collaborative project. Vendors also make customer care calls using conference calls.

Conflicts may exist at any stage of communication with vendors. At some point, you may find yourself dissatisfied with poor service, frustrated with slow response, or upset with confusing instructions. When you are in such a situation, try to take control of your emotions and avoid creating or inflaming a conflict. Focus on solutions rather than penalties (Manifold, 2000). Understand that dealing with conflicts requires patience. In the long term, you need to accept the realities of your situation and move from there (Julich et al., 2003). The fact is that vendors are willing to serve their customers better as they see customers the driver of their business.

Collaboration

Vendor–library collaboration is not a new phenomenon, but its importance has only been widely addressed in recent years. Facing a more competitive market and demanding users, both parties want to move quickly but are constrained by limited resources and expertise – many libraries do not have in-house developers while vendors lack valuable feedback from the front line. They must collaborate to resolve challenging issues and problems that neither party is capable of resolving alone. Through the collaboration, both parties can bring resources and expertise together for innovation and service excellence.

To identify potential areas for collaboration, vendors have to be brought into the context of library collections, services and end-user interactions. It is clear that vendors are not only associated directly with library resource management and service delivery, but also with end-user experience through the products and services they provide. Based on a relevancy analysis, we can identify at least three main areas for collaboration:

- *User studies*: usability testing, usage analysis and user-generated data (tags, reviews, etc.) analysis, and more recently, usage driven collection development and recommendations, etc.

- *Back-end systems*: re-design of the back-end system framework (e.g. Ex Libris Uniform Resource Management) and system integrations, etc.

- *Data services*: enhancement of metadata management and improvement of a centrally maintained knowledge base.

Other collaboration areas may be identified as needed, such as mobile applications, e-book solutions, etc. On another note, the open source community has a lot to offer in support of collaboration. Be open to ideas and potential opportunities.

The landscape of collaboration appears to be very diverse and dynamic. At a community or consortia level, it may be collaborative testing on a beta release; at a professional organization level, it may be developing and implementing new standards; at an institution level, it may be staff training and project outsourcing; at a personal level, it may be co-presenting and co-authoring; and at any level, it may involve collaborative research and development. The collaboration itself may take place in various forms, such as test partner, focus group, task force, product working group, customer advisory group, etc. The collaboration time frame may vary, ranging from a few months to several years.

Although any party can take the initiative, it is often seen that vendors take the leadership role in a large collaboration project, partly because they usually set aside a budget for research and development. Vendors select library partners for a collaborative project based on certain criteria: to help them learn how well they address language issues, regional content, a variety of organizational structures and a range of disciplinary focuses. By being a partner, you commit your time and resources to close and deep collaboration.

It is important to see vendors and libraries as a community, from which any positive contribution will eventually benefit the entire community. This is the real value of the collaboration.

Reciprocal collaboration and growing together

A reciprocal collaboration yields positive outcomes, which can be divided into two categories: measurable and immeasurable.

- *Measurable*: a reduced total cost and an increased number of customers on the vendor's business performance chart, and an increased usage of resources and services on your library annual report.

- *Immeasurable*: marketing and new business opportunities for vendors, expert-level consultation on technical solutions, learning and networking opportunities for libraries, etc.

Vendors usually offer some deals to their partner libraries, such as a discount rate for a purchase or a longer period of trial. They often provide free webinars on new features of incoming products or updates on existing ones. They are willing to do on-site demos if requested. You can take advantage of these offers for the good of the organization and try to turn them into learning opportunities for you and your colleagues.

Doing favors for your vendors doesn't really require a lot of effort. For example, if a product really solves your problems, spread the word and recommend it to others; take a few minutes responding to vendor surveys and questionnaires, etc. You will be appreciated by the vendor for doing so.

After all the effort you have made to build winning partnerships with your vendors, you can expect to grow with them as you move forward together. It is the collective wisdom built on top of the winning partnerships that empowers the collaboration body and ensures mutual success and a bright future.

References

Breeding, Marshall. (2009) *Library Technology Guides*. *http://www.librarytechnology.org* (accessed December 28, 2009).

Ex Libris Ltd. (2009) *Ex Libris: the bridge to knowledge.* *http://www.exlibrisgroup.com* (accessed 28 December 2009).

Gordon, Rachel Singer. (2003) *The accidental systems librarian.* Medford, NJ: Information Today, Inc., 2003.

Julich, Suzanne, Donna Hirst and Brian Thompson. (2003) 'A case study of ILS migration: Aleph 500 at the University of Iowa.' *Library Hi Tech* 21, no. 1: 44–55.

Manifold, A. (2000) 'A principled approach to selecting an automated library system', *Library Hi Tech* 18, no. 2: 119–29.

Wilson, Thomas C. (1998) *The systems librarian: designing roles, defining skills.* Chicago, London: American Library Association.

7

Enterprise computing and the library: managing the transition

John Durno

Recently, Marshall Breeding identified a number of powerful factors driving a transition to enterprise computing for libraries. These factors include security, scalability, better redundancy and backup of critical systems, and basic economics. It is far more cost-effective to build one enterprise-scale infrastructure to handle organizational computing requirements than it is to replicate that infrastructure on a smaller scale throughout a single organization. Equally importantly, a shift to enterprise computing provides an opportunity for the library to participate more fully in objectives important to the entire organization, rather than focus exclusively on its own service mandate. Breeding makes a convincing case that 'for libraries that [...] reside within large organizations, connecting with the broader enterprise network is a vital strategy, both technologically and organizationally' (Breeding, 2009).

Even accepting the essential correctness of Breeding's view, in a large organization it can be a challenge to transition from an environment of independently-operating technology silos to one that relies upon enterprise-scale infrastructure to get the job done. At the University of Victoria, a good project management process was a key factor in facilitating that transition.

When I became Head of Library Systems at the University of Victoria, in early 2006, it quickly became apparent that the unit was under considerable strain. In talking with my staff, and reviewing position and unit descriptions, I repeatedly encountered statements to the effect that 95 per cent of staff time was taken up with maintaining legacy projects and infrastructure, leaving only 5 per cent for new projects and initiatives. At the same time, I was aware that a number of new projects were on the horizon that would require substantially more than the 5 per cent of staff time as yet unallocated.

Hiring more staff was not an immediate option, due to fiscal constraints. So we undertook an inventory of existing projects, to determine whether it would be possible to jettison old project areas for new. Two things quickly became apparent: one, that few, if any, of the existing project areas had outlived their usefulness; and two, a surprising number of them had nothing to do with what could be described as 'Library Systems.' Rather, a very large percentage of staff time was taken up maintaining IT infrastructure common to any modern organization: email, file storage, DNS, DHCP, servers and associated infrastructure, desktop management and the like.

Further, the Library was not alone. While some centrally managed equivalents existed, several other departments on campus had also chosen to implement their own infrastructure. This did not on the surface appear to make good organizational sense. As these services were required by all of the departments on campus, economies of scale would clearly dictate a centrally managed infrastructure.

On further investigation it became apparent that the economics played out differently when considered from the departmental perspective. Historically, the University's central IT group had been focused on maintaining large-scale administrative systems, such as finance, registration, payroll, and so on. Services to departments were often lacking critical features, or came with a price tag that made self-service seem the fiscally responsible choice.

However necessary it may have been at the time, this model was clearly unsustainable. The Library had neither the mandate nor the budget to effectively provide a full range of IT infrastructure services in addition to pursuing its own projects, and in consequence the Library's projects were in many cases not being adequately resourced. Not only that, but much of the infrastructure had been built out of consumer grade equipment and low-end software, the best the Library could afford. An external audit indicated this posed significant risk to the Library's administrative data and operations, as well as significant hidden support costs.

The increasing complexity and cost of running an organizational IT infrastructure meant the self-service model was no longer viable. Fortunately, the Library was not alone in coming to this realization. The need for a radical shift in the provision of enterprise-level IT services had been recognized for some time at senior administrative levels at the University, and a restructuring of the central IT group was already underway. One result of the restructuring was to greatly expand the role of central IT in the provision of services to departments.

It was fortuitous timing for an alignment of interests. For our part, the Library was only too ready to jettison many of its locally maintained IT services if reasonable alternatives could be found, while the central IT department now had a strong mandate to provide those alternatives.

However, even though the strategic direction of both parties was now congruent, the process of transitioning services to central infrastructure still had to be worked out. Since many of the services being migrated were core to day-to-day work throughout the Library, and heavily interconnected, it was clear at the outset that the process would need to be managed in a planned and systematic way, to ensure minimal disruption throughout the organization. A badly managed process would almost certainly cause significant loss in productivity. It could also erode trust, possibly to the point of undermining the entire project.

This became even more apparent after an inventory and analysis of Library-hosted services was undertaken by the central IT group, to determine likely candidates for migration to central support. These included our Microsoft-centric desktop support infrastructure including Active Directory, Exchange email server and file storage, as well as basic networking operations like DNS and DHCP and hosting for the Library's web presence.

It also became clear that, broadly speaking, the migration of Library Systems to central IT would proceed in two streams. The first stream would include commodity IT services common to most modern organizations, as identified above. The second would encompass the hosting of a number of Library-specific applications including a linkresolver, metasearch engine and ERMS. While the same project management process was used to manage both streams, the Library's involvement in that process differed greatly for each.

The introduction of a formal project management process was one of the cornerstones of the restructuring of central IT, and it was achieved through the creation of the Project Management Office (PMO), a one-person operation whose role it was to develop a project management methodology, apply that to projects throughout the central IT group, and promote the use of formal project management techniques through education and outreach. This was fortunate, and reflected a clear recognition that an expanded service model for central IT, including a transition from a departmentally-funded to centrally-funded model for many of those services, would need to be appropriately structured to ensure that the new services were introduced in an effective and equitable manner.

The PMO developed and championed a methodology based on the Project Management Body of Knowledge (PMBOK), an ANSI standard developed and promoted by the Project Management Institute. PMBOK may be considered as a framework for developing project management processes tailored to the requirements of the contexts in which they are employed. In other words, PMBOK represents 'the sum of knowledge within the profession of project management.' How it is applied to any given project or set of projects depends upon what is appropriate as determined by the project management team (Project Management Institute, 2004).

Broadly speaking, the project management methodology employed at the University of Victoria takes a tiered approach, becoming increasingly formalized as the need for resources increases. Very small projects, defined as those costing less than $5,000 and requiring less than 20 person-hours of effort, fall outside the formal process altogether. At the other extreme, projects costing more than $5,000 and requiring more than 40 person-days of effort must go through a process involving a formal charter, plan, and multiple levels of committee approval.

A project in this context is defined as 'a temporary endeavour undertaken to create a unique product or service. It is made up of defined processes and tasks, and has a definite beginning and an end'. Key players include the Sponsor, who champions and is ultimately accountable for the project; the Project Manager, who is responsible for ensuring that the project is executed according to plan; and the Project Team, the group responsible for executing the tasks identified in the plan (Bassi, 2008).

Projects are typically initiated with a Project Charter, which describes the proposed project in sufficient detail that it can be understood and evaluated by those not directly involved. This is sent to the PMO for review, and may be sent back to the initiator for further work if it is considered incomplete. When the Charter has been approved by the PMO, it is sent to the Project Review Committee (PRC), comprising senior managers within University Systems, including the CIO, for review and discussion. If the charter is approved, the PRC may decide to issue either an approval to execute, in which case the project may proceed without further planning; or an approval to plan, which indicates that a formal project plan is required before the project may proceed. In the case of projects requiring significant resources, the PMO may refer the decision to another committee, the Information Systems Steering Council (ISSC), consisting of senior University administrators. In addition to approval to plan or execute, the PMO and the ISSC can assign other statuses, including 'on hold', 'approval in principle', and 'rejected'.

Once the project has been reviewed and approved, it is assigned a formal tracking number and enters the formal project monitoring process. This consists of weekly reports from the Project Manager briefly outlining the project's status, including achievements, next steps and obstacles. The reports are reviewed by the PMO throughout the life cycle of the project, and the PMO may intervene if it appears a given project is experiencing difficulty. Finally, when the project has been completed, the Project Manager submits a close-out report describing what has been achieved, lessons learned, and any variance from the original plan or charter.

Initially there was some resistance within the Library to adopting this process. One of the key challenges of moving the Library away from a locally maintained infrastructure was a perceived loss of independence and the flexibility to adjust priorities in response to changing needs, by staff more accustomed to working with a high degree of autonomy. However, our experience subsequently demonstrated that the overhead imposed by the formalized process has been well worth the effort, in terms of keeping projects on track, but even more so in the substantial benefit accrued from running Library technologies on a well-supported, enterprise-class infrastructure. The time required up front to work through the project planning process was more than recouped after the resulting services went into operation.

As mentioned above, the migration of Library IT to central infrastructure took place in two streams. The migration of the Library's administrative IT infrastructure was given priority over the Library's more specialized projects, for several reasons:

- Centrally supported equivalents for the Library's in-house technology either already existed, or were well along in the development and planning stages.

- The process for migrating departmental infrastructure to central services had already been defined.

- There was a greater benefit to the organization in migrating administrative IT to a centrally supported infrastructure, due to increased levels of redundancy and after-hours support.

At the risk of oversimplifying a large and complex project, the key factor in migrating the Library's administrative infrastructure to central services was the correct sequencing of steps. Broadly speaking, central services had first to be configured to meet the Library's needs, after which all of the several hundred devices on the Library's network had to be reconfigured to work with the newly provisioned infrastructure. Finally, the old infrastructure had to be dismantled.

The initial phase involved provisioning several interrelated technologies. As a first step, new VLANs were created on the University network. This enabled the transition to central DHCP without incurring large service outages. Storage space on the University's SAN had to be allocated, and an appropriate unit-based file structure was created. An Active Directory OU for Library Workstations and Groups was provisioned, and group policies were defined.

The second phase was by far the most labour-intensive, as it involved visiting every workstation in the building, rebuilding users' profiles in the new environment, and manually migrating settings, email, print queues and so on. While there are tools that can automate the migration of users from one Active Directory to another, they do not work reliably in organizations where users have pre-existing user accounts in both AD environments. The only option in such a case is a manual rebuild.

Given that many of the changes being made resulted in visible alterations to users' day-to-day computing environments, communication and training were key. Several information sessions were held for staff prior to the migration, and basic training was provided immediately following the migration of user profiles to the new infrastructure.

Although a significant amount of planning and com-munication was required to achieve a successful outcome; in this case the Library's involvement with the formal project management process was at the resource level. We did not initiate a project charter to effect the transition, but rather conducted our activities as an adjunct of a project already underway within the central IT group focussed on the development and implementation of new departmental services. In that capacity, we had direct representation on the implementation committee, and had further input into the project at the level of senior administration.

Our involvement with the project management process became more formalized when planning for the second stream of projects got underway. Because there was no pre-existing process for the migration of Library applications to central infrastructure, it was necessary for the Library to initiate and manage the projects required to effect the transition.

Experience with formal project management techniques had been limited in Library Systems up to that time, so the outreach component of the Project Management Office mandate was central to ensuring that we understood and could meet the requirements of the process. This involved working closely with the Project Management officer, as well as attending a number of tutorial sessions which clearly outlined various aspects of the project manager's role. Several Library Systems staff attended one or more of these sessions.

Within a relatively short space of time, we were able to develop sufficient expertise within Library Systems to successfully conduct a number of small-scale projects according to the required methodology. These included hosting in the enterprise data centre for three new application servers as well as an upgraded environment for our library catalogue. In each case, project charters were written detailing the purpose of the project, sponsor, scope, schedule, work breakdown, resources required, costs, assumptions and risks. In most cases, projects were granted permission to execute following a review of the charter by the Project Review Committee; in one case a full project plan was deemed necessary before permission to execute was granted.

There were a number of obvious and expected benefits that accrued from clearly delineating project requirements at the outset. Identifying the scope and deliverables helped to keep the projects manageable, and assigning tasks and timelines in advance made it easier to keep projects on track. Although delays and complications were not entirely avoided, most had been anticipated, and strategies pre-formulated for coping with them. For example, alternate staff with the requisite skill sets had been identified in advance, in case one or more of the project principals were unable to complete the work. This contingency planning proved highly useful when a Library systems administrator left to work for another organization midway through one of the projects.

Other benefits were less obvious, but no less welcome, and in fact may have been even more important to ensuring successful results. The consultation undertaken during the planning phase ensured that all of the participants were consulted prior to the projects going forward. This gave everyone involved a stake in achieving the outcome, and ensured that the project could be undertaken in a systematic way. Also, the detailed work breakdown left no uncertainty as to who had the ultimate responsibility for each task. Clear assignment of responsibilities becomes increasingly important in cross-departmental projects where the participants may not be in communication with each other on a day-to-day basis. Finally, the endorsement of the PRC meant that the project had a clear mandate to go forward, and operated with the authority of senior administration in both University Systems and the Library.

Finally, the clear assignment of roles helped greatly to address concerns held by Library Systems staff regarding the transfer of Library Systems work to the central IT group, by making it clear that their involvement was still central to the ongoing success of these projects. Historically, library systems administrators' work had been split between infrastructure and application management, with the bulk of the time being spent managing infrastructure. The end result of the transition to central computing was to shift the balance of their work toward managing Library applications, and as these proliferate and increase in complexity, there is no shortage of work to go around.

Three years after beginning the process, what remains of the Library's local infrastructure? Most of the Library's mission-critical applications, enumerated above, are now hosted centrally. The rest will be migrated as its hardware reaches the end of its life. Mission-critical applications are defined as those where downtime would greatly disrupt day-to-day Library operations.

However, there is still much equipment that the Library maintains locally, and most likely that will continue for some time. On the server side, there are legacy applications where a centrally hosted option is not available. We have a small number of special project servers, whose requirements are sufficiently complex, unpredictable or simply so Library-centric as to make them unlikely candidates for enterprise hosting. We also host servers for development and testing. In both cases, the requirement for flexibility and direct access trumps the advantages of a more robust infrastructure. On the desktop side, Library Systems continues to support hundreds of workstations and other networked devices, with numerous builds and configuration requirements. The work of the Library's desktop support team was least affected by the transition, although it has benefitted greatly from access to a well-supported infrastructure and enterprise-class configuration tools.

Achieving this balance between centrally and locally maintained technologies constitutes the optimal outcome for the migration initiative. The goal was never the simplistic one of moving Library Systems to central computing; the goal was to rationalize the infrastructure so that work could be allocated in a way that made most sense for the University as a whole. It is perfectly appropriate that the Library maintains its own technical staff and infrastructure required for Library projects, while University Systems takes over work that can be more effectively consolidated at the enterprise level.

Access to a good project management framework was a cornerstone in achieving a successful transition to enterprise infrastructure, but it has broader implications as well. Increasingly it has become evident that many other projects within the Library could benefit from a more structured approach to project management, particularly as Library projects increasingly involve collaboration with other University departments. These could include, for example, collaborative projects between the Library and other student services groups on campus; between the Library's digitization unit and Humanities Computing; or between Reference and the Educational Technology group. Even within the Library, collaboration across units works best when roles and deliverables are clearly defined. It is likely that, as librarians increasingly take on project management roles, formal project management techniques will come to be seen as an essential part of the librarian's toolkit. To that end, the Library has begun to plan the adoption of its own version of Project Management methodology, furthering the culture of project management within the University. The benefits of engaging at the enterprise level may therefore turn out to extend well beyond access to better technology, affecting not only our working environment, but our organizational culture.

References

Bassi, N. (2008) *PM Methodology 4.0: Project Management Methodology Handbook*; available at: *cass.uvic.ca/pmo/documents/internal/Framework/SystemsPMMethodology4.doc* (accessed December 15 2009).

Breeding, M. (2009) 'Libraries Thrive Through Enterprise Computing', *Computers in Libraries*, 29(6): 34–6.

Project Management Institute (2004) *A Guide to the Project Management Body of Knowledge: PMBOK Guide.* Pennsylvania: Project Management Institute.

8

Doing more with more: systems, services and emerging technologies

Lisa Carlucci Thomas

Introduction

The modern academic library is a dynamic center of research, education, teaching and learning – a continuously evolving hub of information exchange and technological advancement. To effectively offer these services, today's college and university libraries employ experts skilled in the arts of communication, analysis, information organization and content management; individuals savvy in spotting and tracking emerging trends, mastering and implementing new technologies, evaluating hardware and software, troubleshooting, and balancing the competing demands of quality, quantity, time, service and budget. Behold the systems librarians, poised and ready to take on even the most ambitious or vexing challenges, armed with wits, patience and professional training.

These days, systems librarians are doing more with more: using more technologies, trends, tools, techniques and tactics to meet and exceed the ever-changing information needs of higher education. Systems librarians wear multiple hats; they lend expertise to diverse projects in all parts of the library, and provide leadership for strategically planning relevant and useful technology initiatives. These librarians are an ambitious group, as it is their job to develop and maintain a sturdy systems infrastructure that supports the technological livelihood of academic libraries. This requires anticipating and employing new methods of delivering content, understanding the application of new technologies, and organizing, accessing, transferring and preserving data; all in coordination with the library administration and the information technology partners at their institutions.

Systems librarians have a broad range of position responsibilities and job titles. They are also known as information technology librarians, automation librarians, technology and instruction librarians digital services librarians, technology specialists, web services librarians, digital technologies librarians and more. In addition to varying titles, systems librarians also have varying position duties depending on the size and organizational structure of their libraries. Systems librarians often participate in reference, collection development, technical services, instruction, liaison, research and committee assignments as part of their regular workloads.

This chapter will examine the multi-faceted role of academic systems librarians and explore how they are supporting the systems, services and emerging technologies currently used in academic libraries. 'Doing more with more' refers to evaluating the myriad tools available and selecting and employing those tools which have the broadest impact or offer the greatest opportunity to enhance library services. It is a de facto creed of the modern academic systems librarian, one who navigates the seas of technological and cultural change without veering off-course or off-purpose – that is, to create and support a functional, technologically efficient information environment for students, educators and researchers.

Systems

The constant advancement of systems and computing technology requires that libraries develop or hire professionals able to monitor trends, keep current, identify opportunities, and plan for change. It is commonly known that technology advances in accordance with Moore's Law, and consequentially, systems librarians operate in the context of perpetual change. However, articulating the specific effects on systems librarianship can be somewhat challenging because the role varies widely based on the needs of the employing library. Nevertheless, at the center are the complementary responsibilities of managing library automation and computing technologies. An exploration of library automation history reveals a rich and storied past, which serves as a foundation for our technological present: from the use of analog card catalog technology, to the introduction of isolated support systems to facilitate library technical and circulation services; to networked resource sharing and union catalogs, mainframes and client/server systems, graphical interfaces and web-scale discovery; to research databases, electronic collections, digital repositories, Web 2.0, mobile platforms and much, much more.

The rich automation and systems history of libraries is recorded in part by Marshall Breeding's website, *Library Technology Guides*. This resource focuses on 'key resources in library automation' and provides a comprehensive look at the past, present and future of library systems (*http://www .librarytechnology.org*). Resources include: current industry news; data on the library automation systems of academic research libraries, public libraries and urban libraries; and directories of library automation vendors, library websites and catalogs, and next-generation catalogs. Additionally, *Library Technology Guides* offers links to a wealth of articles, columns and books published by Breeding himself. All in all, this website is an invaluable resource for practicing systems librarians and those aspiring to learn more about the responsibilities of the role. Of particular interest is Breeding's visual guide to 'mergers and acquisitions in the library automation industry,' which imparts unique insight on library vendors, systems and change cycles. Each juncture represents numerous libraries weighing the costs, demands and priorities of systems upgrades; likewise, each juncture represents systems librarians at the ready, able to learn, evaluate, recommend and implement changes (Breeding, 2009d).

Systems librarians are integral to the process of selecting appropriate integrated library systems for their institutions. There are also many tangential assignments systems librarians take on before, during and after a systems upgrade. It is not unusual for systems librarians to be called upon to develop or install support programs to 'float' an old system until a new system can be purchased by the library. This is often necessary because 'running a system beyond its life expectancy can isolate the library from its users, who increasingly expect to experience library services through current-day technologies' (Breeding, 2009c: 20). Once a new system is in place, systems librarians identify opportunities for enhancement, confer with stakeholders to itemize priorities, and plan for future adaptation. Breeding observes that a 'new system, especially in its early versions, lags behind the legacy product it replaces, a product that has had many years to mature' (2009c: 20). Thus, it is the systems librarian's challenge to assess the efficiencies lost in the migration, prepare training documentation and educate colleagues about how to optimize use of the new system.

Beyond management of traditional automation technologies, systems librarians keep an eye on the horizon to ensure awareness of developments that offer promise or opportunity. New systems and interfaces in the forms of next-generation catalogs, open source software and web-scale platforms have gained ground as appealing and viable alternatives to hefty integrated library systems. Moreover, endeavors from non-library specific enterprises, like Google's suite of tools and platforms and Amazon's web services, present untapped potential for library integration. Systems librarians electing to explore such new developments build expertise, define best practices, create knowledge resources, and directly and indirectly improve products in the market for use by future libraries.

Services

Systems librarians provide service to both internal and external customers daily. Responsibilities range from computing support functions, such as technology installation, upgrades and problem resolution, to knowledge enhancement services, such as instruction, documentation, training and assessment. Rachel Singer Gordon, author of *The Accidental Systems Librarian*, outlines essential service skills for systems librarians in her article 'A Course in Accidental Systems Librarianship.' She prescribes four 'courses' necessary for applying 'library training to technology problems in libraries': 1. Organization of Knowledge, 2. Basic Research Techniques, 3. Learning How to Network, and 4. Instruction Techniques Gordon, 2001: 26). She asserts that librarians, by training, have the ability to manage knowledge and information, ask information-bearing questions during a reference (or service) interview, research challenging questions, and apply problem-solving tactics to achieve positive results. Gordon encourages systems librarians to continue to develop and refine these competencies. She also describes the importance of building a network of peers to consult when more experienced guidance is needed, and of honing instruction skills to 'break complex lessons down into small steps,' avoid jargon, and adapt to the needs of the learner (Gordon, 2001: 27).

Communication as service, that is, effective information transfer dedicated to delivering a successful outcome, is the sterling characteristic of a seasoned systems librarian. Andrew K. Pace writes, 'One of the particular challenges in leading a systems department is developing both a thorough knowledge of the library field and an ability to communicate the technological perspective to non-technical staff' (Pace, 2004: 92). Rachel Singer Gordon observes, 'One of systems librarians' most important roles, therefore, is that of communicator – both imparting knowledge and translating technical terms and ideas' (Gordon, 2003b, n.p.). Jody Condit Fagan gets right to the point: 'Communication skills are top priority' (e-mail, March 1, 2010).

Fagan, Digital Services Librarian at James Madison University, shared observations from the field with the author by email. In her experience, she learned that it is important to 'coordinate a process with good opportunities for input' since librarians and library staff members are 'passionate about their jobs' and want to contribute to project outcomes. Fagan points to the success of 'introducing project manage-ment techniques that allow time for this sort of conversation to happen – that plan for it – so it's part of the process' (e-mail, March 1, 2010).

For most systems librarians, clear and managed communications allow for successful hands-on endeavors. From systems-specific responsibilities, such as technology upgrades, networking, web services and troubleshooting, to generalist responsibilities of reference and collection development, systems librarians lead or participate in projects that touch all aspects of the library. Systems librarians have access to available tools for obtaining statistics, generating reports, tracking collections usage, and providing relevant information and feedback to library decision-makers. In addition, systems librarians can often see the 'big picture' due to cross-departmental assignments and can therefore help identify priorities based on overlapping needs. This perspective is especially beneficial as systems librarians develop and manage library-wide technologies, like web content management systems, electronic resources and management systems, digital collections, and institutional repositories.

Emerging technologies

Technological expectations of library users are evolving based on the increasingly social, mobile, interactive and collaborative information environment. Who advises library administration of these changes and ensures that colleagues have the awareness, skills and confidence to test new products and determine opportunities for enhancing library services? In most libraries, these tasks fall under the purview of the systems librarian as an extension of their systems technology and service responsibilities. Within the past few years, specific positions dedicated to the exploration and implementation of emerging technologies have been created at universities around the country, yet it remains to be seen whether these positions will be a passing trend or proven essential to academic libraries. What is known, however, is that in the numerous libraries lacking dedicated positions, the systems librarian steps in, based on their technological experience and ability to master new technologies. An understanding of virtual communication methods and language is of critical importance when considering how to develop an online library presence, or implement a text message reference service. Furthermore, knowledge of web standards, scalability, interoperability, licensing and other digital rights issues is paramount when creating a Facebook page, Flickr account, Twitter profile or other Library 2.0-enabled service. Social networks are extremely useful to libraries as marketing and content hosting platforms, but must be regularly assessed and maintained to maximize results. Systems librarians, familiar with analytics tools, search engine optimization, usability and data management considerations like naming conventions, archiving and version control, apply their technical expertise and library training in tandem when managing library services using emergent technologies. Systems librarians also play an important part in teaching their colleagues how to navigate and use such technologies, and recognize that 'librarians need to be informed about these technologies in order to make decisions about what, when, if, and how ... [they] should be implemented in the library' (Corrado, 2008: 29).

Conclusion

Rachel Singer Gordon writes that those who become systems librarians 'are by personality and by training uniquely suited to adapt traditional library skills to the challenges of integrating and supporting computer technology' (Gordon, 2001: 25). Today's systems librarians apply these talents in diverse ways; they carefully select the best tools from an expanding toolbox of technologies, communicate with partners and stakeholders, and stay up to date with emerging trends in order to achieve institutional goals. It is more important than ever that 'many aspects of automation' – and systems librarianship – 'be re-examined in light of current library realities' (Breeding, 2009c: 21). Systems librarians need room in their schedules for research, development, movement and play, since many new technologies require experimentation to learn (Corrado, 2008: 28). As expertly trained information professionals with technology skills enhanced by experience, successful systems librarians 'bridge the two worlds of technology and librarianship' (Gordon, 2003b: n.p.). Moreover, systems librarians view the past, present and future of library technologies, functions and services in composite. By proactively employing technological tools to support the creative research activities of today – whether planning infrastructure upgrades, designing state of the art web sites, or supporting new modes of discovery and access to library resources – systems librarians are doing more with more, and building a new foundation for the scholars of tomorrow.

References

Breeding, Marshall (2009a) 'Libraries Thrive Through Enterprise Computing.' *Computers in Libraries* 29.6: 34–36.

Breeding, Marshall (2009b) 'History of Library Automation.' *Library Technology Guides* [n.p.]. Retrieved March 10, 2010 from *http://www.librarytechnology.org/automationhistory.pl*.

Breeding, Marshall (2009c) 'Moving Forward Through Tech Cycles.' *Computers in Libraries* 29.5 (2009): 19–21.

Breeding, Marshall (2009d) 'Opening Up Library Automation Software.' *Computers in Libraries* 29.2 (2009): 25–27. Retrieved May 7, 2010 from *http://www.librarytechnology.org/automationhistory.pl?SID=20100314660858154*.

Breeding, Marshall (2009e) 'Social Networking Strategies for Professionals.' *Computers in Libraries* 29.9: 29–31.

Breeding, Marshall (n.d.) *Library Technology Guides* [n.p.]. Retrieved March 10, 2010 from *http://www .librarytechnology.org*.

Corrado, Edward (2008) 'Social Software, Web 2.0, and Libraries. In *Defining Relevancy: Managing the New Academic Library*. Ed. Janet McNeil Hurlbert. Westport, CT: Libraries Unlimited, 2008. 16–31.

Ennis, Lisa A. (2008) 'Talking the Talk: Communicating With IT.' *Computers in Libraries* 28.8: 14–18.

Ernick, Linda (2005) 'Floating Bibs and Orphan Bar Codes: Benefits of an Inventory at a Small College.' *Library Resources & Technical Services* 49.3: 210–216.

Fagan, Jody Condit (2010). Email message to the author. March 1, 2010.

Gordon, Rachel Singer (2001). 'A Course in Accidental Systems Librarianship.' *Computers in Libraries* 21.10: 24–29.

Gordon, Rachel Singer (2003a). *The Accidental Systems Librarian*. Medford, NJ: Information Today.

Gordon, Rachel Singer (2003b) 'Overcoming the Systems Librarian Imposter Syndrome.' *LIBRES: Library and Information Science Research Electronic Journal*. 13.2: [n.p.]. Retrieved May 7, 2010 from *http://libres.curtin .edu.au/libres13n2/index.htm*.

Gordon, Rachel Singer (n.d.) *The Accidental Systems Librarian* [website]. Retrieved May 7, 2010 from *http:// www.lisjobs.com/tasl/*.

Marcin, Susan, and Peter Morris (2008) 'OPAC: The Next Generation.' *Computers in Libraries* 28.5: 6–14.

Pace, Andrew (2004) 'Starting Off on a Technicality.' *American Libraries*. 35.4: 92–93.

Index

Breinigsville, PA USA
27 October 2010
248142BV00003B/1/P